The
Runner's
High

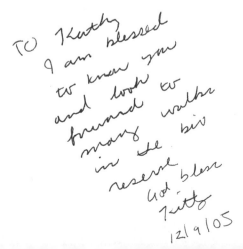

To Kathy
I am blessed
to know you
and look to
forward to
many walks
in the big
reserve
God bless
Kitty
12/9/05

The Runner's High

Illumination and Ecstasy in Motion

Edited by Garth Battista

BREAKAWAY BOOKS
HALCOTTSVILLE, NEW YORK
2004

ISBN: 1-891369-49-0
Library of Congress Control Number: 2004106532

Published by Breakaway Books
P.O. Box 24
Halcottsville, NY 12438
(800) 548-4348
www.breakawaybooks.com

FIRST EDITION

Contents

Introduction 7

The Voice Grace Butcher 11

The Amen of Running Eva Bednarowicz 17

Metamorphoses Handan Tülay Satiroglu 23

The Runner's Gaze Tim Hardwick 29

Coward G. A. Isaksson 37

Strange Fits of Passion David McLean 45

Mind Wide Open Steve Nelson 53

Big Heads and Little Legs Alan L. Steinberg 59

Lines Sara Rufner 65

Cemetery Run Lisa Allen Ortiz 73

From Running to Yoga,
  Finding Your Spiritual Path Brad Curabba 79

Running on Faith Laury Katz 85

Fifteen Minutes (of Fame) Adam Hausman 89

The Miracle Within Rob Hamel 95

The Statue of Liberty Wore Nikes Barbara MacCameron 99

A New Skin Sara Lucarelli 103

Outrunning My Father Clara Silverstein 109

A Run with My Father Leonard Topolski 113

Running to Him Shelley Ann Wake 117

Conversation with a New
  Running Partner Kay Sexton 121

Milestone Melissa Garrison Elliott 127

Soaring Over the Wall	Andrew F. Martin	133
Fireflies	Heidi E. Johnson	139
Maybe Tomorrow	Abigail A. Crago	145
My Daily Tranquility	Leslie Cave	149
How Humans Fly	Dan Sturn	153
Feed Your Head	Katherine Montalto	161
The Ocean High	Pam Gershkoff	165
Sunrise, the Desert, and Five Thousand Years of History	Tracy Musacchio	169
Something That Happens	Stephanie Hawkins	173
Running to Agnostos	John A. Cantrill	177
Eastern Tracks	Ana Yoerg	179
Running from Sadness	Adrian S. Potter	187
Marathon Day: Angels, Chariots, and Isaiah 40:31	Gerry Bell	191
I Could Run Forever	David G. Grant	199
Memorial Run	Carisa L. Heiney	203
The Gift	Chanty Ruth Netting	207
Open Your Heart	Kitty A. Consolo	211
Perhaps This Is Enough	Judy Wolf	215
Running for My Life	Nick Ullett	219
The Way to Fill a Sunday Afternoon	Suzanne Schryver	223
Happy Heart Running	George Beinhorn	227
Running in Circles	Chris Armstrong	233
Knowing Running	David Talbird	237
Finding My Way to High	Mary Z. Fuka	241
Morning in the Garden of the Gods	Gerald C. Matics	245
Penitentiary	Robert Padilla	251

Introduction

The essays in this book reveal the most rapturous moments of running, and they offer clear glimpses of our inner lives. We escape from the tedium of daily existence with the physical exuberance of a good run, and sometimes that simple act is lofted up into something extraordinary. Some people find that the runner's high confirms or augments their belief in God, and that the high is a moment of communion. For some it is simply an enjoyable, if weird, pleasure; or a blissful, timeless meditation. Others find that the sublime joy of the runner's high is a confirmation of something else—a broader spiritual force, or unknown powers within humanity.

As with the parable of the three blind men describing the elephant, I believe that all the essayists here are describing one huge magnificent thing. Each is telling us a distinct truth about it. And what they are describing is not just the anatomy of these uplifted moments, but also something about us all. Humanity's essential physical nature—the animal in us, all blood and lungs and sinew—when used and exercised thoroughly, sometimes leads to a hidden ethereal part of ourselves. We discover that we are built for illumination and ecstasy, but the gift goes mostly unused; it is hardwired in us, just as we have legs to run, but not all humans run.

Reading these essays we begin to sense the nature of this mysterious phenomenon. Given the diversity of voices here, and their wondrous panoply of experiences, I think they may have covered nearly the whole damn elephant.

—G. B.

The
Runner's
High

The Voice

Grace Butcher

We are like spectators at our own events, says Thoreau in *Walden,* in the chapter called "Solitude," speaking of our unique human ability to observe ourselves even as we are most absorbed in what we are doing. And on that night over forty years ago when ten years of intense dreaming had become reality, I had a chance to observe myself in what was the strangest half mile I ever ran.

Running track was the big dream of my life from the time I was— well, I can't remember how old, for I can't remember a time when I didn't run. When I was little, I used to play cowgirl: My legs would be the horse, the rest of me would be me as I galloped through the golden summers, my skinny little body possessed of a strength and endurance that I soon realized was far greater than that of all my girlfriends and many of the little boys.

In junior high and high school I longed to compete in track, but in 1949 girls simply didn't do such things. Finally my mother, aware of my needs and saddened by the lack of opportunity in the schools, got in touch with the legendary Stella Walsh, an Olympic champion and world record holder who lived forty miles away in Cleveland. Did she know, my mother asked, if such a thing as track for girls existed anywhere?

To my incredible joy, Stella herself coached a team and invited me to come and run with them. So for several years I trained with this great athlete although there was still no track for girls in the schools, not even, it seemed, on the farthest horizon. Almost all national competitors came from small ethnic clubs like Stella's Polish Falcons.

I had always dreamed of running the mile; my bedroom walls were papered with photos of the great milers (all men, of course). But in those days girls ran nothing farther than 220 yards. They ran hurdles, did the high jump and broad jump (as the long jump was called then), threw the discus, javelin, and shot, and ran in short relays. Although I became a slightly-better-than-mediocre hurdler, I was not really suited for any of these events. But I knew somehow that if I could just run longer races, I would be the best runner in the whole country. I *knew* it! But how could this dream ever come true when girls weren't even allowed to race around the whole track—when running even a quarter mile seemed about as likely as walking on the moon?

Then when I was a junior in high school, running futile and aim-less laps alone around the gym after class, my behavior incompre-hensible to my peers, I went with a boy on our high school track team to see one of the big indoor track meets featured each winter in var-ious cities around the country: the 1950 Knights of Columbus Meet held at the old Cleveland Arena, long since fallen to the wrecking ball of progress. Ten thousand people used to cram excitedly into that building to see some of the world's greatest stars perform. The track was a steeply banked wooden oval, twelve laps per mile. Sprints, hur-dles, high jump, and pole vault were held in the infield.

The atmosphere was electric, my excitement almost unbearable. The rows of seats, each section painted red, white, or blue, reached from the top edge of the wooden track almost to the very rafters of the arena. In outdoor track, athletes and spectators were spread out all over the field, but here, indoors in the middle of winter with thousands of screaming fans almost literally hanging over the runners as they thudded around the springy boards, the intensity and sound were at a level that swept me away into the wildest fantasy imaginable: to run at this meet someday! Not very likely, it seemed, when I was, so far, just an average athlete, plugging away at events I was no good in, dreaming of running races that girls just didn't run.

But in 1957 a new coach in Cleveland, Alex Ferenczy (recently over from Hungary and amazed at the limitations placed on female athletes in America) and I waged a battle with the AAU to have the 440 and 880 added to the women's national program, and in 1958 I won the first women's half-mile run in the U.S. in modern times at the AAU National Indoor Championships in Akron, Ohio. Progress came fairly quickly after that, and the next year I learned that the Cleveland K of C Meet was going to include the half mile among the few women's events in what was basically a men's meet, This information burst on my awareness like the sudden brilliant flowering of fireworks against the darkness on the Fourth of July.

I had dreamed for almost ten long years of running at that meet. The Cleveland Arena seemed some kind of magical, almost sacred place where athletic gods strode the track worshiped by thousands of cheering, applauding spectators. No one ever seemed to come to the few meets I'd run in so far, but this meet . . .

The Arena was usually sold out for the K of C Meet. As I walked from the parking lot that night, wearing my warm-up suit and carrying my track bag, people tried to stop me. "Got an extra ticket? Hey—got any tickets?" I was walking into the Arena not as a spectator but as an *athlete!* I felt unreal, hyper-aware of the whole scene. It was almost like a déjà vu experience after all my years of imagining it. I felt that curious doubleness that Thoreau talked about, as if I were both participant and spectator at this dreamlike happening: "Now she walks in through the competitors' entrance . . ." The *competitors' entrance!* All these years of waiting!

I warmed up in the concrete corridors crammed with people, hearing the crack of the gun for other events, the roar of applause that greeted each new winner. The smell of hot dogs and popcorn was making me a little sick, the colorful warm-up suits of other athletes swirling and blending into the crowd that we all jogged among, eagerness and anxiety both engulfing me until the impact on my senses became almost unbearable. This night I was not a spectator standing in line for the hot dogs; I was an athlete, running, running . . . soon to jog down the long narrow aisle of concrete steps to the track, pushing aside that dense curtain of sound with my thin, sweaty body, trying to move lightly, strongly, feeling as if all ten thousand people were watching me, *hoping* they were . . . soon to run the half mile (". . . girls don't do that" a diminishing echo soon to be lost forever in the shouts of this crowd and all crowds to come) . . . all these years of picturing myself here, doing this very thing, and now it was really happening. If one could die from an overdose of adrenaline from butterflies rampaging out of control, I should have died then and there.

The Clerk of Course called us to the line, checked us off. Six of us were in this first-ever big-time race. The starter gave us instructions, and the gun went off. I ran a few steps into a dimension I didn't know existed.

Suddenly I seemed to be up in the rafters of the arena, looking down at my race far below. I could see the black framework of the high catwalks vaguely around me, the cables, the great spotlights, the blazing brilliance of the tiny track so far beneath me, and myself running in the midst of the others in my race that was going on both with me and without me.

And in the total silence of this incredible vantage point, a voice said to me clearly, in a kindly sort of way, "Well, Grace, this is what you always wanted."

And then I was back down in my race again, winning it, setting a new U.S. record. Afterward, exuberant, curious, and a little wistful, I asked some friends who were there, "Didn't anyone clap or cheer or anything?" I didn't remember hearing the crowd at all.

"Sure they did! Everyone was yelling and screaming. Didn't you hear them?"

No. I hadn't heard anything. Except the voice. I don't even remember anything about the race itself except for what I saw from up there. But it was what I had always wanted, just as the voice had said. It seems only right somehow that one of the most mysterious, maybe even mystical moments I've ever had came as a part of running: the most rewarding and fulfilling activity of my life beyond anything else I've ever done, one that continues to this day forty years later, and perhaps means even more to me now than it did then. The Running— I always think of it with capital letters—The Running—the truest and most beautiful thing I know how to do.

GRACE BUTCHER lives in Chardon, Ohio. She has been competing in track since 1949. She was American record holder or champion at 880 yards / 800 meters from 1958 to 1961. In 2003 she was the U.S. Masters Champion at 400 meters. She is a Professor Emerita, Kent State University, and editor of *The Listening Eye*, a literary magazine.

The Amen of Running

Eva Bednarowicz

I have never been an athlete. My parents did not let me play sports, so I grew up on the sidelines of team selection, adept only at faking doctor's notes. I taught myself to run later in life out of determined desperation: I *would* reach a finish line without humiliating myself.

But even athletics was easier than prayer.

The way *Time* and *Newsweek* report it, many people are fluent in prayer. But I can no more pray than compel a bat to strike a ball. I am, in fact, bilingual: I can count, write, and curse in both American English and Polish. But, ironically, the more words I know, the more useless they are. I cannot say the word "sports" without imagining both the lunge of muscles and the lungs of a smoker tarred by the nicotine of ancient Polish cigarettes dubbed *Sporty,* yes, sports. Too often it feels like one language is shadowing the other, poised to interfere at a moment's whimsy.

Conversation with God has always been tricky for me. I have always thought that in prayer, piety demands a passionate precision. But it is hard to be precise when you have two languages to choose from, and one contradicts the other because the associated cultures do. It's easy enough to start out by praying in Polish, a dialect of

Catholic lament. But the mind wanders: Often an American alternative will burst in and lob away any humble intention. In the Lord's Prayer, Polish "bread" is just that: bread, the sandwich kind or the kind you queued for, in the days of communist cold. But since I am old enough to remember when "bread" in American English frequently referred to money, sure enough, this connotation intervenes. If I pray in English, which is easier for me now, that's the "bread" I also keep thinking of. If I switch back into Polish, I still remember thinking about "bread" in American English. At this point I reproach myself that I had even thought in terms of profit and not need, but that to me is the nature of American English. It is a language of personal credit and not public deprivation. The result: Praying in Polish makes me sound insincere. Praying in English makes me sound duplicitous. Soon I don't even know what I am talking to God about in the first place, my mind a scrimmage of meanings.

For years I could not complete a prayer. The final resounding *Amen* seemed an impossible marathon away. So be it. So be *what?* How could I conclude when words, spontaneous or rote, could not focus any plea?

And so it came to pass that one Sunday ten years ago in Poland, instead of kneeling in a pew, my boyfriend and I decided to take a run somewhere in the countryside. We trotted down a path that wove through an unknown pine forest. Twigs snapped, birds flapped, and blueberry shrubs shrank away from us as we kept running. The hunched old man who unexpectedly appeared ahead of us on the narrow path should also have known we were coming. Get out of our way, old man, my feet pounded out.

Just as we were right upon him, he stopped, abruptly, and we almost crashed into him. We swerved around instead, momentum interrupted. Some yards down the path, we turned around to look at him with disgruntlement.

He was casting out for the path ahead of him with a roughly hewn wooden staff. It grazed the pine needles and roots in his way like a jagged beam of light. He took the first solemn step ahead. Then the staff shot out again in a clean arc across the path. When he was ready, he took the next endlessly slow, endlessly deliberate step.

We picked up speed to put the old man behind us. We were running away from our own embarrassment and as we ran, as I ran, I heard it.

I heard what he must have heard as we passed him: breaths, breaths in the distance gaining in on him, moving past him, then fading alongside the clamor of feet. He had heard us, all right: He was after all listening because he had to, listening to the gossip of the trees, the cones crackling beneath his boots, and the pulse of his body steering a safe way through the invisible, scented woods.

Over and over again, I breathed.

And as I ran, for loss of all words, only one rang true to me, the lonely echo of all my desultory prayers: *Amen.* So be it. Verily. The single word that began so many of Christ's parables and ended all prayers. A word to breathe by: *Amen.*

That night, and all the following day, I could not stop hearing my breath. It was as if I was still running in those woods and my breath demanded to be heard to the point of obscuring all other sounds and above all, words. Every time I spoke, I caught myself listening for the breath behind the word. But to hear that breath I had to fall silent. I just had to stop speaking and let the breath be. Let it breathe. So be it, my breath.

Then I found myself listening to other people I knew and didn't know. What were *their* breaths like? As I did my usual run, I wondered about all people shuffling past me and wondered, wondered about the shape of their breaths. When I wasn't doing that, I was back to fussing over the odd rhythm of my exhalations like a baby warm from the womb. It didn't even matter that I "finish" my run. It was as it was: I breathed as I breathed.

And in running I heard that breath racing louder than ever and knew it for what it was: a talk with God conducted through listening and not speaking; acquiescing and not asking. An infinite interchange measured by beats of breath more honest than words. Such a compact conversation could be served at the altar or starting line because its beginning and end, its call and response was captured in a single breath *in* and breath *out*. Running honors the breath and focuses it because the breathing accelerates, panting loudly to be honored. What second wind visits us is a just reward for the respect we show for the ones that precede it.

But the breath, I realized, wanted to be heard not just on a path through the woods, but every day from behind the words that it inspires. In thinking to work with breath against words, I was at last conversing with God the way that God converses with the faithful: by listening alone. Hearing. It was the breath that had been ever discreetly praying for me even when I thought my words failed me. I was to trust in breath guiding me to breath, as if all breaths were the counted but countless beads of a rosary gifted to me by my lifetime.

Like the old man on the trail, God hears all intentions ever delivered by our breaths whether we sleep or run. She stands in our way waiting for us to fall silent, listen, and attend. Long-winded petitions may even be welcome, but a simple *Amen* suffices forever.

The coarse languages of my mind, Polish and English, are like two hands that still cannot come together in prayer. But in running, my body has learned to listen to my breath, which, heightened by the run, becomes the offering of appreciation to God. And to God, I am sure, the breathing of Her people is like the rustling of forests. Not a leaf trembles, not a leaf falls, that it goes unheard.

Verily.

EVA B. (for short) has led a multicountry, multicontinental life of teaching and learning. Currently in Toronto, one of the many homes of her youth, she runs the Writing Centre at Humber College.

Metamorphoses

Handan Tülay Satiroglu

No alarm clock today. No beep-beep-beep hammering through my head at the wee hours of the morning. No painfully long commute with its share of somber, mummified travel partners or men rubbing against my body while trying to befriend me. Far, far away from the world of concrete and steel, of wires and wheels and mechanisms, I am under a powerful spell. The spell of the sea.

A ray of golden light steals its way into the room. At the light of dawn, I rise to my feet with the melodic and orchestrated sounds of birds and bees and crickets; the eyes, the ears, the nostrils catching faint whiffs of sea salt on the breeze coming from the balcony door left ajar. Listening to the gentle waves, I look out into the ocean; the landscape pounds before my eyes, jumping out and kissing me tenderly as it is meant to, soothing, appeasing the soul, awakening each and every sensation. I want to dissolve into and become one with this tableau the only way I know how—running—running infinitely, weightless and bodiless on the silken cushion of sand. *At last, here I am, on the island of Langkawi.* I knew from the first moment, a few seconds after my plane landed, I had slipped into these wide spaces, this atmosphere of salt and sublimity, this amazing piece of natural heaven and haven, like a ship gently slipping into her berth. Unable to resist the siren call of the Andaman Sea, I put on my running shoes, gently rub sunscreen on my face, arms, and legs, drink half a cup of water, and set out to explore the depths of nature—my nature.

I begin quietly on the tip of my toes to avoid startling nature out of its sleep, for the first rays of sunlight reveal a sleepy coastline. There is no sign of life. An eternal sensual, I exist in a state of near constant amazement at the immense beauty of my universe. Once again—in solitude and serenity—a far cry from the busy streets of Washington DC. *This* is the real me. Alone first time in weeks and months, to take up my real life at last. Friends, passionate love, work are not my real life unless there is time alone in which to explore and to discover what is happening or has happened. I taste it fully only when I am alone. For five years, running in the streets of the big city, I found myself longing for the solitude and the bliss I had grown accustomed to on the outskirts of the Rocky Mountains. *I had battled every inch of the way to a share of bliss and serenity against the constant drone of existence.* Mile after mile, it was the same agony; people, cars, dogs—the usual relentless assault of noise, speed, pollution. Like dragging a reluctant pooch by the neck, every day I dragged myself to the flat terrain and pavement that hurt my knees and ankles, blistering my feet. *How different I am here* . . . Within my vast solitude, I want to crack open the inner world.

The sun pounding at my temples, pearls of moisture running down my side, there is the sweet and sensuous joy of inhaling and tasting a hundred pleasures of the senses that I had only begun to know. I am besieged on all sides by color; though the first attack came by way of exiting the plane, the greatest assault rests in the moment—the shimmering cool emerald-green water and foaming clouds are a beautiful sight from this run. Sweat spraying from my skin with each foot strike,

I run in the cool haze of my own creation. With each slap on the powdery white sand, my soles absorb the heat that rises like electricity through my arches and ankles and the stem of my shin. It is a carnival of sweet pain, but I love each stride, as it brings me closer to this breathing vibrant mother earth. *How gracious, how benign mother earth is left on its own . . . and yet we live in a world with vanishing beauty, of increasing ugliness; a universe prodded, paved, mapped, and chopped up in an endless quest for the ultimate "civilization."* It might have been Aristotle who asserted that "nature makes nothing in vain." I wonder what gives humanity the right to skin, to deplete, to wreck, and to destroy this lovely planet entrusted to us. What is life anyway, but the flash of a firefly in the night, salt-scented breeze brushing on your face, the whiff of ripe berries in a forest, or the little shadow that runs across the golden sand and loses itself in the sunset?

Here I am, bathed in sweet joy of nature like a rippling pool, beside which the remainder of my life falls into a shriveled, motionless, worn-out daydream; a case of an impoverished soul and body, a shackled servant to the human-made world. So full of thoughts and the echoes of the sounds of water music, suddenly my heart *weighs down* with the longing of a life that *could* have been, and the reality that all that would be irretrievably lost once I returned home. Perhaps, I would spend the remainder of my life trying to find my way back into this state I had fallen into. I would spend many months and days seeking to quench my thirst for that perfect peace, of *being*, of living in the moment unencumbered and liberated. *If only I could live like this forever. What could be sadder than the inability to wholly participate in this life—our infinite capacity to better recognize and understand the subtle coaxing messages picked up by our eyes, ears, skin, and nose?*

Possessed by something between panic, dread, and joy, I begin to leap faster, higher; aware of its ephemeral state, I look more closely, listen more attentively, trying to sense things more deeply. Brilliant rays of orange and gold pierce the sky like beams from a flashlight. I sigh, shut my eyes, and feel the radiant glow inch up my face, my skin rippling with chills at the felt presence of the cool waters . . . Water, water, and more water, stretched out in every direction and as far as my eyes can see . . . I drag my eyes away from the green enchantment and notice a bird dipping into the swirling clouds, reemerging, then tracing back my path . . . The moist, virgin sand beneath my soles squeezes like foam, enveloping, drawing the focal point of my body. A gentle breeze with scent of fresh salt breathes in my face. A vivacious crab weaves in and out of sight as I float through space. I hear only the resounding sounds of my footsteps and my gasping breath. One at a time, migratory birds make their way through the sky. I wonder why they all take the same route in the morning . . . I feel the whole sky in my throat

Flirting with nature, I am doing the beautiful dance, each stride a leap through space. I feel my heels cushioning my return to earth, the toes springing me off again. Half naked, I reach out to the clouds, the wind sweeping across my belly and streaming my hair expressively. *How safe I am here* . . . Running alone on powder, my heart burgeons with a deep and quiet joy, a reverence for life. My footsteps growing even louder, heartbeat pounding like the rhythmic beating of African drums, legs like weightless coiled springs propelling me forward. I am running hard. Against the foggy gray backdrop of my entire life, *this is* the rainbow; this is the play, the energy source, the unstoppable laughter, the outrageous flirtation, the Cup Which Runneth Over. This is the harvest, the generous, excess and gusto . . . To really run is to let go of the constraints of life, to dive deep into the uncommanded, uncontrolled, and uncharted waters of life . . . The old angst-ridden self and world has vanished; instead I am in a fluffy, borderless, weightless, thoughtless world where immersion in the moment reigns. *At last I am waking up and shaking off the grogginess of a long, long nap.* I feel close, so close to this animated and fluid world where nothing is fixed, concrete. Rainer Maria Rilke, the poet, understood this all too well: "Physical pleasure is a sensual experience no different from pure seeing or the pure sensation with which a fine fruit fills the tongue; it is a great unending experience, which is given to us, a knowing of the world, the fullness and the glory of all knowing." I sense a flash of pain on my left shin. *No, not now,* I decide. *Whatever hurts, I don't care.* Soaked, panting, sweat stinging the corners of my eyes; I swing my arms high forward. Wave after wave, happiness gushes over me madly. I am out on the fringes of the out-of-human world, the dazzling water, the translucent skies, the slight breeze drawing me farther out, into the unknown. I sail like a deep-sea diver in a dream, a daydreamer . . . de facto, sensual perceptions leaping out at me, vision narrowed one-pointedness. A feeling known only to those whose strange deviations of the mind take them to an altered state of consciousness, suddenly I see the cloud shadows darkening the large crust turn into frizzy black lichens radiating, shining across the rock's surface; the discarded half-buried tire in the beach transforms into a seal that barks at the menacing foot slaps and galumphs into the water, the breeze rustling the leaves abruptly metamorphoses into a cluster of monkeys foraging for food among branches, gaping with eyes as full as the moons. Nothing here is ever completely certain or fixed; the world shifting and transforming, growing fluid and animate with every glide, every breath, every heartbeat. It is a violent, blood-red, long drawn-out wave of euphoria, and when it is over my spirit will belong to the seashore . . .

HANDAN TÜLAY SATIROGLU is a Turkish American freelance writer and sociologist. She received her B.A. from Colorado State University and her M.A. from New Mexico State University. She currently writes and teaches sociology at Northern Virginia Community College in Alexandria, Virginia, where she resides with her partner and her two cats.

The Runner's Gaze

Tim Hardwick

I used to look on runners with contempt. All that effort spent getting nowhere in particular. It wasn't long before I realized that this perspective was simply a subconscious diversionary tactic, sustained to avert my gaze from my increasingly protruding gut. They had a motivation and fitness; I was a shrewd investor in calories. Sometimes I even comforted myself by imagining how much longer I would survive than others in the event of a mass famine, thanks to my beloved paunch. Homer Simpson, eat your heart out (hmm, perhaps not).

I was twenty years old and already stocking up burnable energy for some future feat of endurance the nature of which I was as yet distinctly unaware. It was the day I caught my best friend taking an active interest in this incessant exercise when things took a profound turn for the better.

It was a fair September morning, much like any other. The summer sun performed its last rites as it returned to the enveloping horizon, and I didn't want to miss the opportunity to soak up its final rays. So I took to lounging on a public bench at the coastal promenade—a favorite venue of mine for jogger-scorning. The long unbroken stretches of walkway proved a popular route for local fitness freaks, and I would idly watch them as they passed me by, oblivious to my unwarranted disdain. I think it was the third or fourth runner to come into my vision that I was forced to allow a double take before I could confirm his identity. It was no other than Nicholas, my favorite and most dedicated beer-swigging partner. I was horrified. My initial bemusement was rapidly swept aside as my mind searched for some sarcastic remark to direct at the poor man when, as if struck by some dreadful moralistic curse, I suddenly felt truly exposed as the languid arbiter of all that was unhealthy. I scanned the immediate pavement, hoping to find a discarded copy of *The Liverpool Echo* to erect between the two of us in the hope that I might not be spotted, to no avail.

But what was I afraid of? Nic just waved and carried on down the path. I watched him and tried to understand the real reasoning behind my dislike for those who embraced the more athletic tendency in themselves, and as he disappeared down the concrete stairs of the breakwater it hit me like a tidal wave: Envy was the culprit. I couldn't stand the idea that others had more zest, more energy to offer life than I had ever been able to muster. I promised myself things would be different from then on. And, to my happy surprise, they were.

The following day I bought a solid pair of running shoes as a symbol of my resolution. Soon I was out of the house and on that stretch of coastline whenever I saw the opportunity, sometimes running with Nic, more often alone. And it is one of those solitary occasions I would like to relate, a time I found myself involved in a remarkable transformation that has affected my outlook to this day.

I awoke to watch thin beams of sunlight making their implacable invisible travel across the bed linen. I got up and opened the curtains. To my surprise I was struck by the sensation that it was summer; the illusion was maintained by the double glazing that stood between the outside world and me, warmth within, cold without, the affair broken asunder only by the exhaled mist of morning walkers below. I was impressively alive from a slumber that usually infiltrated the later hours of waking day. I could already sense my run would be an enjoyable one, and I spared no time in dressing for the exercise ahead. Within minutes I was at the doorstep, working my tendons against the brick wall. It was cool but not uncomfortable and there was only a hint of wind, so I went on my way in the direction of the calm seafront.

After an hour or so I returned home for some lunch to quench my body-fuel need. As I sat down to enjoy French bread and cottage cheese I could already sense that I would run again that evening. My physiological reaction during the morning's excursion had been coolly euphoric to the point where any notion of a division between my body and mind seemed absurd. Every stride I took characterized a feeling of weightlessness that permeated me entirely. Without losing my bearings along the coastline I had the impression I was running not only beside the water but above it also. The sea spanning out to the horizon gleamed and sparkled intensely, as if it were tinged with a saline mercurial dye, and I felt I could see farther than I ever had before. Recalling it with wonder between mouthfuls, I duly looked forward to returning to my travels.

Although the daylight was beginning to wane toward evening, the influence of the sun remained deceptively strong. When I ventured into its beam again I felt I could go on indefinitely without feeling jaded from my earlier run. Certainly, it was as if I now personified a boundless vitality whose constitution resembled an awakening from a deep sleep. It grew in intensity as I continued on.

I jogged into a hazy field, and the soil beneath my feet was bumpy but yielding to my tread. The grass was glazed with dewy icicles, and the effect within the jurisdiction of the hedgerows was that of a sparkling field-length sheet of glowing arabesque; a silver-and-yellow latticework partitioned the vegetation and the crisp air. I was surrounded by colors that looked as if they had never been seen before and were only now, as I lent them my gaze, becoming truly real. Their virgin hues pierced the transparent atmosphere and were an almost audible cacophony. My pupils were pinpricks in the intense ray that shone from everything, and as I slowed my run in fascination I came to recognize almost no division between me—my body—and what was around me. Moving on through the gates to the promenade I detected aspects of myself in the wood used to construct the fence, in the moss covering the breakwater. What had previously resembled a haphazard covering of marine life over the concrete now followed some inspired yet indecipherable pattern that I was somehow a part of.

As I cut across the beach inlet small movements between the ridged thoroughfares in the sand caught my eye. Winding tributaries of anonymous life veered in every direction. Oval silhouettes of compacting salt emerged beneath every foot tread, and I peered behind me to see my wandering wake in the ever-changing tapestry left by the ocean waves.

On returning to the walkway I skipped up to the edge of the seawall like a feverish child and peered into the black riled waves. Hidden life undulated in the rhythmic water below, and with it death. The cold maelstrom allowed no eye to pierce its surface; if fear of the unknown could physically become manifest it was here, before me, welling up the dark unfamiliar images of aquatic terror within: the Kraken, shark, terrible stinging jellyfish, and the silent gulping horror of the solitary drowned.

Yet none of it fazed me. It all somehow took its place in the scheme of things. I stood back from the concrete bulwark and regarded the stars, now brightening imperceptibly. The evening sky was clearing and I saw glimpses of the zodiac, but the harsh inner-city blaze cut out what I knew was overhead, the vast scatter of the galaxy since beginningless time. Still, I appreciated what I could see and considered the tremendous cosmic dome in view, the exposed state of my own nervous system twinkling, the glistening reflection of consciousness. I laughed at the darkening sky, proclaiming my joy to its gargantuan compass. It was a wondrous night.

In direct contrast to the coastal traffic route, the road back into town was still, the air inert, but my response to these surroundings remained transformed. Opposites reflected each other in novel and surprising ways. The breakdown of the separation between my self and my environment had shifted toward an insightful reflection on the seamless relationship between everything around me.

My roving attention was like a slow dance of lights. Up ahead I noticed an old-fashioned pub façade at a crossroads. The grand Tudor building and surrounding trees were incandescent with the eerie atomic green of an anonymous floodlight, and the moon directly above was phased at such an angle as to give the impression it was looking down at the scene in a leaning, animal-inquisitive gaze. It was a picture of strange splendor, and I looked hard at the face of the moon and its eyes and mouth and sensed its amber complexion as if the sodium glare of these innumerable streets had tainted even its remote and cratered countenance.

I ran on, ecstatic. The streets were warm with inconceivable excitement. A busload of students rattled passed with the unknown electricity of nights-to-be.

I was very much aware of the contrast of scenery on either side of me. Cars droned by on one side, while on the other they were replaced by unrolling rustic greenery. I stared at a nipple of land in the distance, a solitary hill, framed through the close irrigation of sky by leafless spangled branches. Sheep munched the fertile grass, content. The dark clouds above parted and, as if in defiance of the night, soft-red dying sunlight poured through the hole like a draining cup; it creamed the hillside and warmed the subdued cattle. The shades of nature vied for distinction in my eye, and every one made its mark. While I physically traveled along the macadam surface, I also found myself on the hill watching my slow direction over all things. Silently I reminded myself of the marvel of existence.

Closing in on home I heard the lazy chime of the local church tower drift over the chimneytops, and I remembered that tonight was the seasonal retraction of the hour. The clocks would go backward and crystallize their pretentiousness, sown by the hands of man. These cycles of life perpetuated their cold impasse in the eyes of humanity, but I was awake to its relentless charade, the lies of nine o'clock and the objectionable grandiosity of midnight. I laughed warmheartedly as the eternal Now constantly renewed itself and forged in my mind the truth of the great temporal fallacy and, smiling, I turned homeward with the warm blood pumping in my ears as if it flowed audibly on the passing wind.

I could have gone on forever. A little later I settled into my bed reluctantly, still beaming from my experience. My thoughts were sharp and crystal clear. If this was madness, I envied the psychotic. To run with no fixed destination in mind seemed to afford a strange sense of release from the hustle and bustle of everyday life. I had found purpose in purposelessness, and it was freedom.

The whole episode had an effect that lingered on for many days thereafter. Frequently I found myself taken aback by all manner of usually lackluster and uninspiring facets of my everyday life. The next morning I arrived at the train station to get to work. I strolled to platform six, stood behind the waiting line, and gazed up at the enormous steel umbrella enclosing Lime Street station. Inside the vast corrugated dome I detected a strange grayish gaseous air that ran all the way down the platforms, and it yielded a supernatural luminosity that made the signalman at the station's opening glow with a ghostly radiance in the seeped-in sunlight.

And once again it all reminded me of the silver sea lapping at the end of my street in the still truth of the illuminated moon.

TIM HARDWICK was born in Liverpool, England, in March 1981. Tim began writing short stories when he was eleven, while his older brother, Jared, would draw the pictures. Tim went on to gain a first-class honors degree in English and American Literature at the University of Gloucestershire. He is currently studying for an M.A. in literature at the same institute. Tim is twenty-three years old, and still running.

Coward

G. A. Isaksson

My education in the merits of suffering began early in life. Being my father's eldest son, I was charged at a young age with the job of mechanic's helper, which usually meant holding wrenches with hands numb from the cold of the winter days his well-used trucks invariably saved their worst breakdowns for. Spending countless hours soaked with cold had its payoffs—I wore T-shirts on days where the temperature kept most people indoors, my first hint that coping with stress was something the human body could learn.

After high school, I competed as an amateur boxer and discovered the discomfort that comes from bringing the body to its physical limits. Once accepted, I was able to handle this type of suffering exponentially, so that what I once shrank from became routine. Running gave me a graduate degree in this course of study. Each distance has its own brand of hurt, and I'd compare the varieties to what I might have experienced if I'd stayed in boxing longer. The burn at the end of a 5K felt a lot like the third round of an amateur fight; I imagined the slower, more thorough pain of the half-marathon being like a ten-rounder. The marathon was a championship. A few miles of feeling things out, maybe even playing the crowd for a while, but slowly and certainly I received a taste of what Muhammad Ali once described as being as close to death he could imagine.

One particular race a few years back, however, stands apart from the rest. I experienced more pain than I ever had before and, though I no longer have the trophy they gave me for winning, I carry its effects with me still.

My hometown firehouse holds a five-miler every spring, and that year I'd done everything right: I endured the soreness from the long runs and aches from the track; I turned up the resistance on my exercise bike and fought the pedals until my legs rubbered. But that's only part of the reason I won. The last hill on the course, between miles three and four, is the other. It's a devil that stares you in the eyes for a half mile; a devil that makes the flatter, faster alternatives being run that day more appealing to the best of our local runners. I reached this hill, along with one other runner, trailing no one. After a hundred yards, with quads on fire and air coming in rapid explosions, the steady, reasoned voices hard effort brings started in my head. These were the same ones I'd learned to ignore in my boxing training, but was never able to conquer in the actual fights. *You don't need to win this race,* they argued, *second place is fine.* Even as I battled them, I wished for the other runner to pull away, but he did something crueler. He fell behind.

Halfway up, there's a ten-yard tease where the hill levels off, but you get around a bend and it's back in your face again. That was when those voices started screaming—something they'd never done before. I pressed harder, letting the pain soak through me like the cold had done when I was a boy, until pain became not something I felt, but something I was.

There's always an ambulance parked at the top of the hill, next to the clock for mile four. When I got there the footsteps behind me were gone. Firemen cheered and the devil hill slowly let go of my legs as the road went flat. Ten seconds later the firemen cheered again, but I didn't turn around; I ran harder, slicing up that course and breaking the tape with a five-mile PR. If the clocks were accurate, that last mile was the fastest I've run in any race. Mere data, however.

I don't talk about what happened after the firemen's cheers drowned out the voices in my head and the courage to win took hold. For the first few strides I focused on moving forward as fast as possible. After that, I can't recall thinking about anything. As I ran, a lightness spread through me in degrees, until it became much like the opposite of the pain I'd experienced on the hill. I firmly believe that if I'd had the presence of mind to look down at any point during those five-odd minutes there would have been a gap between my running shoes and the Earth. For that short time there was only light, along with a feeling I'd experienced once before: a feeling that it was, indeed, a fine thing to be me.

I'd always suspected what I was; one afternoon in the fifth grade I became sure of it. A boy on the school bus punched me square in the mouth and I could only sit there, the pain of the many eyes and their laughter worse than that of my bloodied, swelling lip. Only later that night, in my bed, could I stand and defend myself. Fighting had always been a mystery—I'd never fared well in schoolyard skirmishes—but in my wide-awake dream my hands were smart and the crowd on the bus watched with admiration. From that afternoon on, my school life consisted of many of those little deaths Shakespeare wrote of, interspersed with the purgatories that were the punishment of surviving them. Sometime between that first slow death and graduating from high school to a gas station, I'd seen a professional fight in which a boxer fought three rounds with a broken arm. The fighter began taking tremendous punishment and the referee stepped between the two men, waving the fight over. Walking back to his corner, the fighter shook his head, as if there was something more he could have done to avoid defeat. That memory lingered, and between fill-ups I dreamed of living such a noble, courageous life.

After many attempts, I summoned the courage to walk into a boxing gym and tell an old man with a pancake nose I wanted to be a fighter. He looked me up and down; I expected him to laugh, but he didn't. "Come Monday. I'll start you then," was all he said. Three years of Mondays later I'd learned how to block, slip, and hit, but my greatest asset as a fighter was something the old-timers called "heart," which meant I could take a good shot and remain standing. Of my twenty-five amateur bouts there's only one worthy of mention.

I'd done everything right that year: endured bruises from daily sparring and the dead-arm ache from endlessly pounding heavy bags. The fight was a tournament semifinal and despite the crowd swarming the floor I entered the ring on steady legs. The videotape of that fight always surprises me because it shows what took place but not what *happened*. That night, as I stood sensing the muscles of the timekeeper's arm flex to strike the bell, I felt as if my body was ascending. When I looked across the ring I towered over my opponent, pitying him, because I knew he had no chance to win. The bell rang and he came toward me, pity soon becoming admiration, respect, love, even, because I knew he was going to try, nevertheless. I watched myself jab him to the ropes, land a right to his ribs, then saw the crowd groan in unison, as if they had been hit, as well. Who I was for the rest of that fight—the fighter in the ring or the "other," watching myself perform as I never had before—I'm not sure.

I was never able to recapture the magic of that night. I had three fights after that and lost them all. I quit boxing, leaving my demons behind. I had the flattened nose and scarred forehead as badges of courage, but found I still needed the competition and self-induced suffering I'd become addicted to. Running provided both, and through that suffering I created the athlete who stared down that demon hill and was rewarded with the mile of his life.

On a cold November morning six months after that golden mile, I raced another five-miler. I was in the second pack and we got to the top of a hill, a baby compared to the one in the first race, and the wind hit us dead on. I saw the guys in front, minutes ahead, and the voices started, but this time I listened. I'd felt it coming for some time; a switch inside had been flipped, constructing a barricade my pain would no longer cross.

I jogged to the finish, watching the second pack disappear, then age group winners pass ten years at a clip. That was four years ago and I haven't run a race worth a damn since. I still beat most people, for whatever that's worth. I even won a 5K last fall where they gave me a trophy inscribed 2003 CHAMPION. But no matter what I try I cannot cross that barrier and knowing that has caused the forgotten, familiar suffering of self-discovery I'd learned as a boy.

I think it was winning that got me. Looking back at my boxing, I realized that I'd never been fighting to win, only to prove I wasn't that fifth-grader on the bus. I was content to be a fighter, win or lose. In running, I got trophies that said I was faster than most; faster, surely, than those kids on the bus. For once, I had battled to win, yet nothing was any different. Those kids could still laugh. Pushing thirty, I was still changing oil in that same garage. I still had no direction in my life.

Once in a while I'll read a piece in a magazine where some *writer* is throwing around their bullshit about runner's high, and about their goddamned endorphins way too easily. They make it sound so *nice*, like it's some big tea party where the admission is always free. But nothing worthwhile comes without a price, and I swear when I read that stuff that if I had whoever wrote it nearby I'd show them what I haven't forgotten about boxing. They never talk about the other side, about what might happen when you get to the top of the hill and can only look down on where you're going and where you've been. Running tore away what boxing built, holding a mirror to the flattened nose and the scar, making me realize that they weren't badges of courage, but shields I used to hide a fifth-grade boy who couldn't rise from his seat to defend himself. And now, in every race I run, there's a point where I become that boy again, dying the same languorous death.

Last fall, when I came home with that trophy, I thought back to the defeated boxer with the broken arm and wondered if he'd ever won a belt or if the only championship he ever won was that over his own pain as, for a few moments on a hill, I had done. Perhaps that is the only one that's important. I cleared my shelves of their meaningless plastic and empty medals. I knew what I was, what I'd always been, but it was easier to build a trophy case than a life, so that's what I did, hiding behind those new shields with my serial insecurity and fear of change.

A few months ago a friend sent a poem written by Marianne Williamson that starts, "*Our deepest fear is that we are powerful beyond measure. It is our light, not our darkness that most frightens us.*" It sits in a frame on a shelf where the trophies used to and sometimes I'll read it repeatedly, trying to decide if it's true or not. I'd like it to be but, then again, I don't know if trading one kind of fear for another makes any difference at all.

G. A. ISAKSSON lives and runs on Long Island, New York. His fiction has appeared in various magazines, including *Running Times* and *Struggle*.

Strange Fits of Passion

David McLean

Strange fits of passion have I known:
And I will dare to tell,
But in the *runner's* ear alone,
What once to me befell.

—William Wordsworth (slightly modified)

My father used to scoff at the idea of a runner's high. He dismissed it as a fabrication, a myth, a media concoction, an advertisement. He'd run a lot of miles himself and had never felt the high, or so he said, though I consider this absence more a failure of language than a lack of feeling. His own running began in the early 1950s and ended a few years before Jim Fixx published *The Complete Book of Running*, and I suspect at some point during those years he'd experienced what would later be called a "runner's high." He simply didn't have a phrase for it, and even when he finally did, it was too late. I once tried to explain it to him, to defend the cause, but I couldn't convince him. I couldn't quite capture that sense of blank exultation or that elevated joy that could suddenly make a labored run painless or turn hard work into easy fun as the body rang its own pure tone.

My father was a soldier, a career marine, and running had been many things to him—the suffering of boot camp, a way to stay fit as a Golden Gloves boxer, a tool for tormenting young recruits on the drill field—but it was always a means to an end, a job to be done, not something done for physical pleasure or spiritual enjoyment. Which is perhaps a way of saying that though he'd run a lot of miles in his life, he wasn't really a runner. What running he did do ended abruptly in December 1972. He was a fit thirty-six-year-old gunny sergeant and while out jogging one afternoon he fell over with a heart attack and nearly died. He never ran again. He walked sporadically, rode an exercise bike on occasion, and eventually stopped exercising pretty much all together.

So, given his pragmatic view of running and his disbelief in the runner's high, he would have been amused to know that he was a primary cause of the highest high I have ever felt as a runner.

The run took place in October 1984. I was twenty years old and studying abroad in London, England. Dad was forty-eight and was preparing for surgery on the heart that had betrayed him twelve years before. I'd been in Britain for some six weeks when he had the quadruple-bypass. I was having the time of my life, exploring the city, running its streets, and drinking its beer among innumerable other pleasures. I'd also been having wild, guilt-driven dreams powered by the fear of Dad's dying. On the day of the surgery I was in the Lake District as part of a required classroom weekend involving walking and poetry among the mountains and lakes. The days were so full of scheduled activity that I didn't even pack my running shoes for the trip. I certainly didn't expect to have the run of my life that weekend.

We were in Grasmere preparing for a tour of Wordsworth's Dove

Cottage when I called home to get news about dad. It was 3 A.M. back in southern Illinois, and my mother sounded exhausted over the poor connection. I don't remember the details of the short conversation. I mainly remember watching the digital numbers reel down as quickly as I could feed in the thick fifty-pence coins and the frustration of trying to concentrate on the conversation at the same time. But the important words came through loud and clear: "Dad's just fine," Mom said. "The surgery went great. He says don't worry and keep having a good time."

I nearly collapsed in relief. Weeks of tension drained out of me and the feelings of guilt receded. I got my good-byes and greetings in just as the last pence drained off the display, and I rejoined my classmates. We dutifully toured Dove Cottage and afterward hiked into the hills above, stopping to eat our packed lunch at a little tarn above the famous cottage. A green slope dotted with white sheep rose high behind us.

"I'd like to see the view from up top," I said as I finished my lunch. I was thinking of taking a side trip up.

"We don't have time," said our guide, a pleasant, but somewhat serious bearded Englishman. "We've got to get moving."

I looked up the steep green fell and then back down at the guide. I don't know what possessed me. "I can be up and back in twelve minutes," I said. I don't know why I picked that number. I guess my runner's instincts and experience had unconsciously done the necessary math. I was only a year beyond an organized running career that had lasted three years of high school and two years in college. I had quit my college cross-country team the previous fall after yet another painful bout with shin splints, but three weeks earlier I'd run the best race of my life—five miles in twenty-six minutes flat—and though I was no longer in that kind of shape, I was still pretty fit.

The guide laughed. "I don't think so," he said, polite but dismissive. "We'll see."

I took off running. No matter that I had just polished off a ham and cheese and cucumber sandwich and a bottle of juice, no matter that I was wearing tight blue jeans, an old pair of running shoes, a thick pocketed vest, and carrying a camera. I was warmed up from the hike up and cocky enough to go for it. I didn't like having my running prowess questioned back then.

But I started too fast, attacking the run furiously and stupidly going straight up the slope. After about a minute I felt spent and jokingly fell down on the grass, throwing out my arms in a dramatic gesture of exhaustion. I heard the laughter below, but I quickly got up and began running again, slower this time, more measured, zigzagging at a steady, mechanical pace designed to methodically eat up ground.

I stopped looking down and around and looked up instead—at the rocks, at the sheep, at the grass, at the horizon above me, at the gray sky. Something stirred the old racing heart, and two minutes later I'd found that wonderful place where the runners go when the body and the mind meld together in a kind of empty and wordless elation.

As with all steep climbs, I seemed to reach the top multiple times. I'd think I was there and then a little bit of new horizon would rise beyond, but I kept up my gentle switchback pattern, kept the legs churning, the breath moving, and my eyes locked before me.

And then suddenly there was no more hill to climb. I was at the top of a narrow, grassy ridge that quickly sloped out of sight down the other side. I looked first at my watch—just under eight minutes used—and then I looked around for the first time since clicking into gear.

It was an astonishing sight: a green and glorious country of undulating mountains and ribbons of road and the steel-colored Irish Sea in the distance. Villages nestled in the valleys, and autumn colors burned the edges of the silver lakes. Stone walls crisscrossed the hills, and clouds in every shade of gray rushed quickly overhead. I could have looked at it for hours, but there was a race to win, so I gave myself exactly one minute to drink in the view, snapped a couple of photos, and headed down.

And there I found glory.

Running up had been hard work, the beautiful and painful pushing of the body that every real runner loves and that promotes the runner's high. The descent was my reward.

Something snapped, or broke, or let go, or was born as I started down that mountain. Something exploded: I went mad for a few minutes. Forget the safe S-curves now. I headed straight down, on the edge of control every step of the way. I wasn't just running; I was galloping over the grass, leaping off boulders, bouncing and skipping, using every means possible to maintain my fragile balance. When I felt myself bending forward and out of control, I simply jumped high and slid down on my hip as though stealing second base, flashing through damp grass and slick mud and pebbles of sheep scat, and when I again regained control, I would pop up and dash forward so fast and straight that I felt like a boulder bouncing down the hillside at the mercy of gravity alone.

I had been experiencing the runner's high to differing degrees for years—the competitive fire of the big race, the quiet pleasure and solitude of running during midwinter snowstorms, the roaring of the mind as the legs churned like steam-driven pistons on hot summer days in the sultry Midwest—but this was something different. This was no longer running; this was flying. When it wasn't flying, it was freefalling. This was not the body at play; this was the soul in full flight; this was the spirit escaping the prison of the flesh for a few vigorous and heady moments aloft. My mind was empty of all thought, but the combination of emotional release at my father's health, the physicality of running, and the sublime scenery took me to a place I'd never found in all my years of competitive running and have not found since.

I did once find an equivalent: eleven years later I stood on the deck of a boat off southern California and watched some three or four hundred dolphins frolic almost madly in the surf near Anacapa Island: their feverish natural joy struck me as the perfect metaphor for the runner's high, and recalled that bolt down the fell years before. I was a dolphin dashing through the surf that Saturday afternoon; I was a windhover riding on rippling waves of air.

I made one final slide, coming to a stop back where I'd started near the tarn. I lay in the grass gasping and laughing out loud. I knew I'd won, but I looked at my watch anyway. "Just over eleven minutes," I said through my laughter.

My classmates looked at me as if I'd lost my mind. The guide seemed slightly troubled by this mad American frisk down his green and peaceful mountain. And they all had the same question written on their faces: *What was that?*

I could only keep laughing and look up at the sky. How to explain such ecstasy? Strange fits of passion have I known, indeed: Wordsworth would have understood immediately: the spiritual soaring, the brief flight from the body, and then the inevitable return to the mud and grass that now stained my jeans. I wanted to take that feeling that October day and give it to my father across the ocean, to help him feel better, to make him understand, maybe even to recall a lost moment from his own experience running.

But I didn't have the words, so I said nothing, to my classmates then or to my father later. And even had I found the words, I suspect they would have fallen on skeptical or disbelieving or uncomprehending ears anyway. Such things must be felt to be fully understood. Such intensity must be experienced. And such moments are best told in the runner's ear alone.

DAVID McLEAN is a freelance writer living in Slovakia. His fiction has appeared in the *Atlantic Monthly*. In 2001 he went on a nine-hundred-mile hike through Slovakia, and currently he is writing a book about the journey.

Mind Wide Open

Steve Nelson

The runner's high is an act of remembrance. And forgetting. It's a matter of opening up. And closing down. It's everything and nothing at once, the rapture of motion and falling mindlessly back into nature. Running is something we've done instinctively, intuitively, since we were able to stand on two feet, both in our own lives, as children, and as people in our aboriginal days. To survive in this world, to thrive, our ancestors had to run to find things, to avoid others, to get from point to point. We ran without thinking about it, like children do today. First you walk, then you run. Why is this? Rarely because there's anyplace you need to get to that soon. Children run because it feels good—they chase each other, they race each other, but these are just excuses to run. Sometimes they jump forward because they can't help themselves, because a stretch of lawn is just too tempting to walk across. Runners know this urge, though like children we don't always understand it, thinking we want to exercise, get in shape, get our time in, when all we really want to do is run.

Why is it that the idea of a walk around the neighborhood bores me, while the notion of a run over the same streets enchants? If we can answer this, we're on our way to understanding the runner's high, or the runner's mind at least. A walk, you see, is easy, and though your mind is free to wander, the problem is it doesn't wander far enough. We control the wandering and it never gets too far. A run, on the other hand, requires concentration, and in an experienced runner the mind and body learn to work together, with a concentration that becomes second nature, and allows one's mind to wander in a different way, forgetting the thoughts at the top of the mind and going deeper, toward a more essential version of the self.

The only thing I know for sure about the runner's high is that I can't describe it. Anything that can be described and understood logically is not it because it's as mysterious as love, as life. It's greater than running, though not the reason we run. I'll try to tell you what it is, how it happens, but first I'll tell you what it isn't.

First, it isn't a long run, the one when you want to stop but don't, the run on which you keep yourself going, legs aching, minutes or miles to go, and you want to stop but keep on going on, all the way to the end. Of course you feel good about yourself, for being strong and not weak, for persevering, but that's satisfaction, not the runner's high. Second, it's not a hard workout where you get the times you set for yourself, be it mile repeats, quarters, or just running your regular route faster than ever before. That's a good feeling, too, but it's contentment, a favorable view of both the past and the future.

The runner's high exists in the present, but it's not as simple as that, feeling good, light, energized, the feeling that your rhythm is a little quicker than normal, your stride a little stronger, your breathing easier. On days like this you may feel so good you say to yourself, *I wish I felt like this every day*, or, *I wish I was racing today*. Usually you accept the run for what it is, a gift, a treat, a run to be enjoyed, but this isn't the runner's high, either. And it's also not succeeding in a race, winning, beating your rival, or getting your goal time. This is a great feeling, but this comes from knowing you've worked toward something and accomplished it. The more you've invested, the better it feels, but still, that's not it, that's not *it*. While all these experiences are sublime in their own way, and they make up the catalog of memories we take away from a life of running, they aren't the stuff of the runner's high, and we know this because we can put these experiences into words, and we do, we can't help ourselves but talk about a great race, a long run, a tough workout. We want these known somehow. Is there anyone you don't want to know about your best race?

Your longest run? Our accomplishments, we feel, should be noted. To a large extent, they make up who we are in life. But the ecstasy that comes with the runner's high needs no audience, can have none, and when you feel yourself caught up in it the last thing you want to do is say a word to anyone, initially because it would break the spell, later because you know you can't put it into words, and I realize now that when we're experiencing the runner's high we don't even realize it, it's beyond our comprehension, and it's really the afterglow that we enjoy, the fresh memory of it. But even this, for the most part, we keep to ourselves because we know no one could understand. How could they, if we don't understand ourselves?

So what is it then? Well, now that I've admitted I can't explain it, I guess I'll try. I've got nothing to lose, right? To put it simply, one's body and mind must be working together on the run and must be doing so unconsciously. Let's imagine there are three states of mind. The first, the top, is daytime mind, which is continually jumping from point to point, thinking about what needs to be done next, tasks, appointments, et cetera. This mind is full of everyday thoughts, the ones that occupy us from morning to night and get us through our days with some sort of order.

If you engage in a project and focus on it, leaving the concerns of the daytime mind behind, you've reached the next state, which is the concentrating mind. In this state you are focusing on one thing and the concerns of the daytime mind are (temporarily at least) blocked out. In the case of the run, you might be telling yourself to breathe in and out in rhythm, to lift your knees, pump your arms, to breathe in and out, to flip your ankles and swing your elbows, to keep your rhythm, to keep it going. This is usually easiest after you've warmed up some, you're physically warm, and most of your daytime thoughts have run through your mind two or three times already. Your initial store of energy is gone and in order to keep pace you must force yourself into the concentrating mind.

On most runs then, even a hard run or a race, try as you may, you fall out of this state and back into your daytime mind. You may not be having the same thoughts as before, but after a while you find you're not concentrating on the run anymore. Maybe you're admiring the scenery, or wondering about things you don't really care about, things you didn't know were even in your mind. This happens because it's hard to keep it up, concentrating, running hard. It's much easier to slow down and think about other things, avoid the pain, so you fall back to everyday mind and a slower pace out of self-preservation, which is not a bad thing necessarily, but sometimes, you see, the things you've learned can stand in the way of the things you know, and if you back off every time it begins to get hard, you'll never get through, you'll never make it to the state of the runner's high.

Of course, it's not as easy as simply running through the pain. Running through the pain typically leads to just more pain. But if you do it often enough your body adapts, gets stronger, and more important learns to trust what your mind is telling it. If you reach this state of self-trust, you're ready to move on to the next level, running with deep mind, where the runner's high takes place, and though I've called it deep mind you can also call it infinite mind, pure mind, essential mind, whatever you want, because no words can accurately describe it; words are a part of our daytime mind and they don't exist deep inside us.

You reach this state of mind only after you've gone through the concentration state, and instead of drifting back to your daytime mind, you fall in to deep mind instead. This can only happen on a day your body has energy, enough stored to let you be unconsciously confident in your ability to keep going. So you do keep going, and though you're not concentrating anymore, actively, the concentration is still going on, the run is still going on as before, the concentrating mind and the body are fused together fulfilling the tasks of the run, breathing, rhythm, arms, legs, feet, all in rhythm. You feel it going on with no conscious effort from you, it's going on and on, along with other necessaries such as following your route, crossing streets, avoiding traffic, all this continues without you thinking about it, your body is doing the running but you're detached from it, just along for the ride, that's the last conscious thought you'll have before falling in, losing track of your pace, your path, the time of day, even your name and history, you lose it all and exist only in the run, in the moment, moment by moment, and this is not the same as when your mind is focused, which limits your view, rather, it's a matter of open mind, a mind that's nowhere and so everywhere at once. This is the mind of the runner's high.

Though I've described this in stages, you can't control it, where your mind goes. Trying to get to deep mind, of course, is futile because the very attempt requires the use of daytime mind. To get there you've got to let go, and you can't let go until you've trained the body to trust the mind, the mind to trust the body, and even then you don't always get there. Most times you just run. It's a rare day you go beyond, very rare, but it happens sometimes, you know it when you get back; running along and snapping out of it, you realize you've been gone, that you've moved over time and space, and the feeling then is different from what you've just gone through, lesser in some ways, but greater in others because you can appreciate it, the feelings of joy, pleasure, buoyancy, completeness, the almost electrical surge of all this pulsing through the body. You're usually still running when you snap out of it, and you may smile, or raise your hands in exaltation because you feel so good, you know that something grand has just occurred, and you're glad.

But, of course, it goes away after a while, the good feeling, it dissipates over time, and you may ask yourself, *What happened? Was that really me? Where did I go?* I say *inside*, though I could be wrong, nobody knows for sure, maybe it is just satisfaction that makes up the runner's high, maybe it's chemical and can be explained away, but I like to believe that the greatest things about us are the mysteries about us, those things that can't be explained, like the places we go sometimes when running, the places we go.

STEVE NELSON lives and runs in Milwaukee, Wisconsin. He teaches writing classes at the University of Wisconsin–Milwaukee. His work has appeared in *The Cream City Review, eye-rhyme,* and *Phantasmagoria.*

Big Heads and Little Legs

Alan L. Steinberg

Despite the way we look at birth, with our fat little legs and pumpkin heads, running is an essential human activity. The basic sport, as it were. The purest. The simplest. The most human. The most biologically natural. Forget all the hype about air cushioning and orthopedic correctness; running is the cleanest and the simplest kind of athletic activity there is. You're born to run—just like a horse, or a dog, or a cheetah, for that matter. The only difference is, we can't do it right away. Our lives don't depend on running the same way an antelope's life depends on it. Or a wildebeest's. There's no herd we've got to keep up with. No long migration for a drink of water.

So, we're born pretty much unfinished. Big heads, little legs. Wonderfully developed vocal cords to whine and cry our way to salvation. Otherwise, we're pretty helpless. Pretty stationary. But that's the beauty of it. We go from whining infant to waddling toddler to gold-medal sprinter partly by nature, but mostly by will and determination and intelligence—the big-head stuff. Biology gives us legs and hearts and lungs and adrenaline, but it's intelligence and discipline that give us focus and training regimens—and the courage to stay with them. I once read where an Olympic coach said that 90 percent of us are physiologically capable of running a four-minute mile, but in all the world's history only a relative handful ever have. Why? Because biology takes you only so far—to the starting line, in a way. What brings you to the finish line miles away—miles up grueling, side-stitching hills and down skinny, mud-rutted trails—is a combination of all that makes us uniquely human: planning and practice; self-love and self-loathing. Inner fortitude. And that wondrous capacity to let our minds take us where our bodies can't go—out there somewhere between earth and heaven, where gravity loosens its sullen grip and the solar wind becomes a cooling breeze.

Think about it. Think about all the mental gymnastics that go on in a five-mile run. Or a ten-miler. Or a marathon. Nothing is quick or imminent. It's not like a sprint. Not like a hurdle—where everything is technique and coordination and balance. You don't kneel in your blocks and look up and see the finish line. Or hear the cheers and applause. Feel the restless anticipation. No. Everything is still far in the future. Far out of sight. Far ahead of you. Miles and miles away. You've got to imagine it all. Imagine yourself a half hour later. An hour later. Three hours later.

Whatever the distance, whatever the time, you've got to will yourself from here to there. There's no crack of the pistol and then a deep breath and away—then over before you breathe again. You have to imagine the miles, the hills, the wind, the pounding of your heart and feet. You have to imagine the roar of the crowd, because almost always there will be no crowd. Nothing but you and the pavement or the grass or the dirt or the sand.

Running—long-distance running—is mostly not a stopwatch-watching, I-beat-you-to-a-pulp sort of thing. Mostly, it's a spiritual thing. Once you get in decent shape, running becomes a meditative experience, but without all the self-consciousness and even phoniness those words bring to mind. When you get in shape; when you get so your breathing is deep and even, when your legs are muscled yet loose at the same time; when you're moving light and lean, like an energy-efficient running machine, through some pine-scented forest, bending low up a steep hill and then leaning back and letting the gravity that's crushing your bones draw you down the other side, your mind just floats along—taking in the sights, taking in the sounds and smells, taking in the powerful rhythms of life; making it so you become one with the universe, with the earth and wind, with the sunlight and shadows. And for a little while, at least, you put death aside and concentrate on the pure spiritual joy of living.

But there's mystery to running as well. At least for me. Because I never know when that runner's high will kick in, when all of a sudden the ground will give way, along with that egotistical sense of myself as a separate entity churning along the beaten path, and I become instead a living part of it all. I can never tell what sets it off. Or turns it off. I've run through pristine forests and still found every step a self-conscious agony. I've run beside rivers, lakes, and oceans—sometimes in the very best shape of my life—and still my head was weighted down with pounds of worries. And I've been on the dirtiest of city streets or carbon-filled highways when all of a sudden whatever it is that happens happens and I'm in that state again. Not out of myself, but rather in myself so deeply that I go through myself and back out into the world again. I'm aware of everything— and it's all in perfect, if tenuous, balance. The ground makes its demand on my body, but my body is up to it. The hill is steep, but it's exactly equal to the stride my legs make going up it. The wind may be against me, but the pores of my skin seem to open wide enough to let the wind enter and not impede me. All is fluid and in flux. As the color white is not the absence of color but the presence of them all, so the things about and within me. All there. All per-fectly balanced. Perfectly blended. A harmony of the spheres, so to speak, only on a small scale. Everything caught and held in perfect balance. Like a mathematical equation. Like a rare jazz session. Ebb and flow. Drift and sway. Even my thoughts—each one perfectly counterpointed by silence. Every meaning finding its correspon-dence. A worry mated to a hope. A regret side by side with an expectation. An ending exactly at the place where a beginning begins. I leap when I should and land where I must. The muscles in my head, like the muscles in my leg, are just strong enough to bear me.

But just as I never know for certain when it all will happen, I can never know for certain when it all will end. If the trail becomes one degree too steep for my heel or calf; if my heart falls behind a single beat; if the wind shifts before my lungs can compensate—all, then, will break down. I will become conscious of insistence, of the pull of things, of the world and my own small place in it. The harmony will be broken. I will become full again—full of myself and my sad little dreams and desires. I will become old or fat or tired or slow. It will all be give and take, then, all will and consciousness. Weight instead of weightless. Relativity instead of harmony. Importance and insis-tence instead of counterpoint and balance.

But, still, the grand thing about all this tenuousness is the tenu-ousness. A run that begins in misery can turn into something dream-ily spiritual. And one that begins in wonder can end in lamentation. There is no certainty. And yet, in a world that has but one exit, this indefiniteness is what, to me, gives running its grand appeal. I never know how the running will go, whether it will be full of weight or weightlessness, full of gravity or soaring, until I'm done. Until I'm dry and cool and back in the harness again. Still, in this earthbound world we live and die in, there are not many things we do that bring us such uncertain yet all-encompassing joy. We were not born with fat little legs and great big heads for nothing.

ALAN STEINBERG works at SUNY Potsdam. He has published fiction (*Cry of the Leopard,* St. Martins Press) and drama (*The Road to Corinth,* Players Press).

Lines

Sara Rufner

I. Discovery

I've always resisted sports that require a lot of gear. I'm not into hovering in the corner of the garage to run degreaser through a bike chain or, in the winter, iron wax on skis. I'm into putting on my shoes and going. If anything's going to break, it better be me.

For a long time, I ran a few days a week, when San Diego's bright afternoons lured me outside. But sometime that changed, like my stride lengthening over puddles on a wet morning. I can't say exactly when it happened, but how. Slowly, I wanted more minutes in the sun, more of the way I felt breathing and pushing and sweating hard, more of myself entirely spent. I began running past my turnaround point at the end of the beach wall, continuing to the jetty and through the park; at the other end I passed Crystal Pier's warped planks and pushed ahead to Tourmaline beach. That was a rush, like passing through a brick wall unscathed. My metronomic forty-minute, five-mile route, now stretched out a bit on either end, became a fifty-five minute, seven-mile run.

I hovered around the seven-mile mark for quite a while, but one weekend I couldn't resist finding out what ten miles felt like, and the next weekend fifteen, and on some long run, although I couldn't pin down exactly when, either I discovered it, or it discovered me.

It was a high, a super power over exhaustion, a noiseless and unfeeling calm, a seeming separation from my body, a rapturous control, a continuous surge carrying me, and a feeling that I was carrying the surge and in control and out of my body and calm and powerful and hoping this would never end.

It was endorphins.

Those little brain chemicals I unleashed were discovered first by neuroscientists searching not for the source of my runner's high, but for the cause of opiates' highly addictive qualities in the human body, Aptly, they named their find an amalgamation of *endogenous* (meaning "in the body") and *morphine*. Today, I am told, we know more: endorphins are triggered not only by long runs, but also by stress, pain, pregnancy and labor, sex, acupuncture, chocolate, chili peppers, music, and even laughter; and they produce analgesia, calm or euphoria, and even exploratory and creative behaviors. While the endorphin story remains somewhat a mystery, so far there is a lot to like about the body's natural opiate.

II. Pain

Unless I'm coming off a day or two of rest—which I don't do well—I dread the first thirty minutes of my run. Cold, stiff body. Toes still numb from morning caffeine. Neck vertebrae don't absorb the shock as they used to. Muscles clench around them. As I ease into my usual pace, I dangle my hands low so my shoulders will roll back and relax. I bend my head slowly from side. I move the bra strap away from my neck and readjust the waistband of my shorts. My calves feel overstretched, my quads weighed down. Every step I feel the lingering, nagging bruise on my left foot. The airway through my nose is dry and stuffy. The hair around my face blows into my eyes and mouth. I feel pain. I have a long way to go. I look at my watch. Four minutes. Six. Ten.

I don't notice any of it subsiding, except my toes becoming hot and swollen as blood pumps into them, forcing open the thin, constricted vessels. Most of the time I just realize the pain has left me. The stiffness in my calves has melted and the deep bruise on my left foot has disappeared. My shoulders still feel scrunched in a shrug, but I don't care anymore. Sweat rolls down the backs of my arms and then cycles out of every pore, giving my skin a cool, wet shine and pasting the flyaways around my face to the sides of my head. I taste runny nose, clear and salty like ocean spray, on my upper lip. My forced gait has slipped into something natural, my quads now loose and my feet turning over and over each other effortlessly and without any thought as to whether my stride is too long or too short because I don't care, I just like the way it feels.

This easiness lasts at least a couple miles, more if I've been training hard. And then it slips away, or rather the pain begins to slip back into me. It's a different pain but it finds the same vulnerable places in my body. A heaviness presses down on my body the way too many gray days burden my spirit. My shoulders reach for my earlobes. My forearms ache in their right-angle swing, and my pumping hands become clammy, cool, stiff ends. My hamstrings contract, resisting the length of my stride. Sweat-soaked shoes and socks turn my feet white and wrinkly and gnaw on the calluses where the ball of my foot meets my big toe. My turnover continues at its pace but low and sloppy now, the tread on my shoes almost grazing the ground. If my laces are too loose or too tight, my toenails jam against their cuticles.

My wet bra chafes my breastbone. I notice joints—first knees and then ankles, sometimes hips—jolting and grinding. As blood shunts to the core, a pervasive chill seeps from my digits into my limbs. A slow deadening finds even the strongest places in my body.

In times like this, the body knows what to do: make an analgesic until the stress subsides. Endorphins rush into the bloodstream.

I want to stop, oh, I want to stop like nothing else, but the steady shush, shush, shush of my feet on the pavement and the cadence of my breath in out, in out, in out are like a song that never ends. *Inertia,* I think. *I am the ball in motion that stays in motion.* I keep going. I keep going. I keep going.

III. Euphoria

With my calves spasming and the skin under my nose chapping and my right patella twinging and my small intestine contracting and all my muscles thirsting, I run, and suddenly I feel as good as I've ever felt.

I don't know what it is, a trance that has seeped into me, an unlikely combination of power and calm. I withdraw from the bikes and walkers and surfers and dogs passing on the boardwalk and people barbecuing and drinking beer and watching football on their patios, from the cheering and barking and rapping and talking, and enter some other realm, a straight and narrow line.

The line is an electric flow, a silent but live current that has been there all along, and after so many miles, finally I have stepped into the right place at the right time with a few of the right kind of strides, carrying me into this line or this line into me. It passes through me, a thread somewhere in the torso, and I am fixed to it, traveling straight-away and focused while everything around me becomes white space, nothing but the margin of my reality; even my own body is separate from my self, which has entered another sphere and become invincible to continue this easy flowing movement that no longer resembles the striving called running, and I will dwell in this euphoric state for as long as it continues which I hope is forever.

And then the line snaps. A veering bicycle. Or a trio of bikinis strutting side by side with no place to pass. I feel the margin—movement and sounds—encroaching and I force myself to look straight ahead, shut out the noise, and stay focused, as if somehow I can control whatever is controlling me, this power that is suddenly very fragile and all at once, gone.

This, I am told, is runner's high.

And this, I am asked: peace or power? Joy or invincibility? Effortlessness, calmness, spirituality, flow?

What is flow? This, I tell you, willfully resists terminology.

IV. Creativity

I have finished my run and I am bent over, my knees loose, my arms dangling, and the end of my ponytail brushing the ground. Blood floods into my head as I stretch my hamstrings and then my calves. I feel the happiest I know how to feel.

I imagine that my stopping takes all those circulating endorphins by surprise. Lost without the presence of pain, they have nothing to do but flood my emotional reservoir.

In these slumped-over moments of hard-won elation, suddenly something comes to me. A thread that connects seemingly unrelated thoughts, or an answer to a problem, or conviction about something I said the day before, or an impulse to do something. I know what I must write next or what I must apologize for or where I must go. It always surprises me, and I always wonder whether it's chemicals or God suddenly telling me how to live my life. I like to think it's a combination of the two: that God made the switch in our brain that turns them on when we need them. I've learned not to ignore these thoughts, dare I call them revelations, when they come to me while stretching or showering or whatever I am doing immediately after running.

This flicker of the bulb in my brain, I am told, also goes off when I complete a crossword puzzle, find the path of an overgrown trail, or write a turn in an essay. If I were a scientist, I am told, a neurochemical discovery would cause a flicker, too. But right now, bent over, I am doing none of those things. I am totally immersed, lost to self, and satisfied. I know in this moment after running, this is as productive, as focused, as sensitive, as spiritually aware, as good as my brain will ever be.

V. Addiction

The day I cannot run, or somehow feel my blood and breath pulsing as if running, is a difficult one. I am crabby. My coffee gives me a headache before I can drive it out of my system. I am tired but can't sit still. I don't want to be around me, and no one else does, either. After two days of this, however, I feel surprisingly better and my need to run actually begins to wane. These moments of lethargy or rest, depending on how you look at it, scare me more than the withdrawals I feel. What would happen if a third, fourth, and fifth day passed and I never ran again? It's too much to consider. Debilitating injuries that could force me into a state of inertia terrify me the way artists have nightmares about losing their hands.

So it goes, the parallels between opiate addicts and long-distance runners deprived of their usual mileage—depression, irritability, insomnia—discount the idea that runner's high is merely a psychological boost. While the human body cannot become addicted to endogenous chemicals, something turns my passion into fear and my fear into impulse. Something makes me lace up my shoes and go, even when no part of my body feels like running.

I stand with one foot in a place that is good for me and the other in a place that is too good, and I am never sure which foot is holding my full weight and which one is there only for looks. I believe that someday, though, I will realize I am no longer straddling this edge. I will find myself on the right side, the good side, like a runner who has sprinted across the finish line, euphoric.

SARA RUFNER lives, runs, and writes in Anchorage, Alaska.

Cemetery Run

Lisa Allen Ortiz

I used to run through a cemetery. I lived in an edgy neighborhood in Oakland, and Mountain View Cemetery was the closest scenic loop. My cemetery loop crossed a few bridges, meandered along a creek, had two gratifying hill climbs and a long tree-lined avenue that ended in a fountain, perfect for a midrun sprint. I loved that daily run, made it the joyful spark of my weekday mornings. For me, the cemetery offered a bucolic respite from the daily urban grind of my neighborhood. The cemetery was orderly and green, fenced and well groomed.

I took the man who would become my husband on that run, and he was quiet the whole way. "You do this every day?" he finally asked. "Don't you think about all these dead people?" No, I never thought about dead people.

What did death have to do with me? I was twenty-three and talented, athletic, headstrong. Life was a landscape I ran through. Headstones and family monuments whirred by with charming lift and bounce. The cemetery was my loop: I enjoyed it for the hills and shade, the curving paths, the bursts of flowers, the open fields of close-cropped grass. No, I never thought about dead people.

Ten years later, a battle with cancer changed that. The day I was diagnosed with thyroid cancer, I felt abandoned by my former life, my light and springing steps, my runs that were an affirmation of living: All that seemed far away, ridiculously hopeful in a world that was cruel. Suddenly, death was all around me. I felt as though I passed through some cancer door and into another room. It was the cancer room, filled with people waiting. Suddenly my peers in life were no longer triathletes and health foodies; they were people just out of radiation, people scheduling chemotherapy appointments, people with scars and sickness. And I could see, from this cancer room, another door—a door marked death. Like other people who have been diagnosed with a terminal illness, the door didn't frighten me. I just accepted it. I sat, soft and stunned in the cancer room, and simply accepted my view of that door marked death. My husband was frightened by my attitude, but even his encouraging words couldn't wake me from my dreamy and accepting state. *I have cancer*, I thought. *I might die; I might not. There's nothing I can do but accept the treatment allotted me.*

Thyroid cancer is generally considered easy to cure. "If I had to get cancer," one doctor told me, "I would choose thyroid cancer." Treatment for thyroid cancer is standard: Remove the thyroid and any surrounding tumor and then take a therapeutic dose of radioactive iodine to burn out any remaining cancer cells. Because I was breastfeeding my baby daughter, I asked for a few weeks to wean her between my surgery and my radioactive iodine dose.

But in those few weeks after my thyroidectemy the remaining cancer cells in my neck got, as one oncologist later explained "unusually aggressive." One night while brushing my teeth, I saw lumps in my neck. I scheduled an extra check-up. My neck was filled with tumors. The thyroid cancer had spread to the lymph nodes. There was too much cancer to effectively treat with radioactive iodine, and the proposed solution was something called a modified radical neck dissection.

It's a surgery most often performed on elderly men with severe throat and neck cancer: smokers and drinkers. The incision goes from the back of the ear to the base of the throat. They would remove the lymph nodes, the jugular vein, and a muscle called the sternocleidomastoid.

I got second and third opinions to see if this surgery could be avoided. "Don't I have some choice?" I asked. One elderly doctor put it bluntly: "Well, you could die." I was in the cancer room, and I had my hand on the door marked death, jiggling the door handle.

The day before this surgery was scheduled my in-laws took the children so my husband and I could have some time alone. My husband asked if I was up for a run. I couldn't bear to say no. My shoes were dusty, lined with spiderwebs. My neck was still weak from my first surgery, a little wobbly, but I could still nod. Sure, why not? I would give running a try.

We chose to run in Nicene Marks Park in Aptos. My body ached and felt bent and old, ruined, shot through with scars and injuries. I doubted I could really run. Perhaps we would walk. I girded myself for disappointment. I had given birth to two children born with complications. I had a bout of melanoma. Now I had metastatic thyroid cancer. My body had disappointed me over and over again; I could not expect it to hold up now, running up a ridge. But I would give it a try, prove to my husband that I was not completely broken.

Nicene Marks is a ten-thousand-acre strip of park that follows Aptos Creek and then climbs to a series of ridges that look down at the sea. It was brutally logged in the 1930s and '40s, but it has grown back furiously. To leave the bustle of the coast and enter Nicene Marks is to enter a cathedral of redwoods. Beneath the grandeur of those beams of trees is a verdant understory of sword ferns and madrones, firs and bay trees, wild blackberries and huckleberries. At the deep bottom of this cathedral, Aptos Creek twists with elfin joy.

Sitting on a fallen log in that environment, putting on your running shoes, is both humbling and elevating, the definition of spiritual experience.

The climb up the ridge was difficult. I didn't walk, but I am sure I was an unappealing sight as I struggled to run. My lungs heaved and my legs burned, but the oxygen above the creek was nearly liquid, and I persevered. My husband ran ahead of me, and I sank into his stride. I ran and thought about the cancer room, how all summer I had been waiting in that room, transfixed by the door that said death. But I wasn't dead. I was running. I was climbing a thousand-foot ridge, lungs sucking this forest's generous oxygen. I kept thinking about how it must have looked here one hundred years ago, after brutal logging, how locals must have wept, thinking their world despoiled, ruined. But, stubborn with life, the forest had grown back thick, green, and abundant with affirmation. My feet kept moving, rising, stride by stride up, my ankles brushed by the trilliums and lupines that cheered like spectators along the path waving little flags of blooms. Redwoods and firs stood deep and thick beside the path: Old souls whispering encouragement. I huffed up the hill, fighting my tight and tired lungs, but surprised at the will of my muscles, the strength of my bones, the fight that shot out of me like breath.

And then the path rose over one more hill and topped the ridge, became a loping singletrack, and there, spread out like a flag, was the ocean. My husband smiled and let me pass, and I ran. I really ran: light and fast, the ocean sparkling down below my left leg, the forest rioting with life on my right. I was not in any room, not waiting for a door to open. I had escaped. I leaped and sprang like some deer, not fearful, though, not forgetting, just running because running is the best way a body can travel: light and free, animal wild. I was tough, irrepressible, had a head full of lactic sparkle, happy as hell.

Oh, it has been a punishing loop, but I am heading now to my favorite part: the joyful sprint between the trees, home to my family, home to bright mornings and cool afternoons, here on this riotous planet that waits outside any door I care to open, a planet that unrolls before me in verdant, joyful paths.

LISA ALLEN ORTIZ runs, writes, and looks after her fine husband and two wild-haired daughters in rural northern California.

From Running to Yoga, Finding Your Spiritual Path

Brad Curabba

"When we step out of the battles, we see anew, as the Tao te Ching says, with eyes unclouded by the longing."

It was over ninety degrees and I was approaching the hill again. It was the third lap of a five-lap course around the hilly grounds of my high school campus. My breathing was becoming labored and my legs were starting to feel the effects of the incline, my knees were smarting from the decline and my body was telling my mind to slow down.

The outside effects of my internal laboring were obvious: heavy breathing, profuse sweating, and aching sides. Despite these strains and signs of fatigue, my internal body was taking steps to alleviate the discomfort. As the lactic acid in my body was seeping into my muscles, my pituitary gland was busy producing endorphins and serotonin. These chemicals would act as a natural painkiller, and counteract the damage that the lactic acid was doing to my body. I would soon feel the effects, as my breathing began to normalize and flow evenly. The pain in my side and in my knees disappeared and all I could see was the horizon.

My eyes seemed fixed in the distance, no longer concerned about the immediate future, and my pace quickened and flowed, as if I were gliding on air. My sore feet did not painfully react to the constant pounding on the asphalt; it seemed as though my body had ceased to be of importance. My mind had, in effect, taken over. Each stride was joyous and freeing, a smile crept across my face, and I felt for that moment a great universal connection. I felt as if I were synchronized with nature, my breath leading the way.

I felt, at once, that I could run forever. The distractions of finishing well, quickly, left my mind. I was running with a friend and he could tell something had changed. I remember I could breathe and talk at the same time, with ease, and I started spouting out the virtues of Buddhism and meditation, professing that I would one day devote my life to the spiritual. Strange as this may sound, it becomes stranger when I think back on that moment. I was young, eighteen years old, and in no way knowledgeable about Buddhism or matters of the spiritual world. I can only explain it as it has become apparent to me now, many years later. There is a Sanskrit saying, *"Mana eva manushyanam karanam bandha mokshayoho,"* which means, "As the mind, so the man; bondage or liberation are in your own mind." It is an innate, intrinsically beautiful potentiality, which created the feeling of connectedness that I felt during that first experience of runner's high. I was, for a fleeting moment, in complete and perfect balance, my mind and body and breath acting together in a perfectly choreographed symphony. In effect, I was able to find liberation of mind through physical exertion.

This is not at all uncommon for runners to experience. Yiannis Kouros, a legend in the world of ultrarunning, was quoted as saying,

Some may ask why I am running such long distances. There are reasons. During the ultras I come to a point where my body is almost dead. My mind has to take leadership. When it is very hard there is a war going on between the body and the mind. If my body wins, I will have to give up; if my mind wins, I will continue. At that time I feel that I stay outside of my body. It is as if I see my body in front of me; my mind commands and my body follows. This is a very special feeling, which I like very much. . . . It is a very beautiful feeling and the only time I experience my personality separate from my body, as two different things.

The question becomes: What can we do with this experience? How will or should it change our lives or help us to realize the benefits of recognizing the connectedness between our body and mind?

Since that first experience with runner's high I have continually found myself in search of a more sustainable detachment between body and mind. What I have come to realize is that the feeling I experienced during that specific moment of physical exertion can also be attained through contemplation, meditation, and breathing exercises. Yoga, like running, is a way of achieving this end.

This result, and subsequent way of life, is especially important in modern-day America. To achieve awareness or calmness of mind is important not only to live a happier, more meaningful life, but also to block out all of the negative influences that we find ourselves surrounded by on a daily basis.

The constant violence, suffering, and deception that we see on the evening news cannot help but create within us a feeling of fear and anger, ungratefulness and hatred. All of these feelings add to the already seemingly endless wave of negativity that our society seems to generate on a daily basis. The ultranationalism and xenophobia that exist around the world are a result of the continuing search for external pleasures. Increased trade, increased profits, cheaper labor, faster and more advanced technologies may help us accumulate more material wealth, but in doing so we are alienating the spirit. We, everyone, have ceased to place importance on finding peace within, and the results have been increased violence abroad, and increased unhappiness at home.

Our modern societies have also created a massive sense of detachment and denial. We live in a society in which we are closed off from the truths of existence, and fill the void with substances to ease the fear of the inevitable. Anne Wilson Schaef, author of *When Society Becomes an Addict*, describes it this way:

> The best adjusted person in our society is the person who is not dead and not alive, just numb, a zombie. When you are dead you're not able to do the work of society. When you are fully alive you are constantly saying "No" to many of the processes of society, the racism, the polluted environment, the nuclear threat, the arms race, drinking unsafe water and eating carcinogenic foods. Thus it is in the interests of our society to promote things that take the edge off, keep us busy with our fixes, and keep us slightly numbed out and zombie-like. In this way our modern consumer society itself functions as an addict.

We can begin to effect change if we can understand these truths and work to become aware of our surrounding and the workings of our society more clearly. If we begin first with ourselves, whether it be through running, yoga, mediation, or prayer, to become more aware of the powers that our bodies and minds hold, we will be able to live in a more peaceful way. The powers of concentration, patience and the breath are important and valuable tools in the war against suffering and the continuing violence in our world.

BRAD CURABBA lives in New York City, where he teaches English as a second language. He enjoys writing about travel and international affairs.

Running on Faith

Laury Katz

It begins as all sacred things do, a calling of sorts, from a voice foreign to the ear but all too familiar to the heart—and you rise to the calling because you know where it leads, you've been there before and long to return. Paced, steady, breath in tune with each graceful step, awakening the spirit with each tranquil breath. It's the beginning of a song, the slow build, the longing to join hands with the part of you that can only be found when your head is clear, and your feet can no longer distinguish the pavement from the very air you breathe.

Encompassed by the subtle smells of earth, the awakening builds. The body's pace quickens, as does the breath, enabling the spirit to continue its quest for freedom. The legs begin to rise to the occasion and aid the feet on this journey, as they bend with poised purpose— lifting the feet higher, moving us faster, with grace and fluidity. Arms follow suit, bending and swinging swiftly through the air—they are guided by instinct and do not cling to their work, never boastful or in need of recognition. The body has transformed itself: no longer flesh and blood, but rather an instrument, played softly by the air that whispers, *join me in this dance, let me lead you and twirl you and dip you slow.* But we are skeptical, and gradually the breath begins to shorten, and the pace slows as we tire in anticipation of the physical demands of the journey. The whole process disrupted like a great chorus building at the hands of the conductor, then suddenly—a string is broken, a voice is cracked at the threshold, the energy flow has been interrupted, and the choir is in disarray. The conductor is aware but composed, wanting desperately to return to that place—she gathers the power of their voices in her hands and they build again—with relief and renewed hope.

The breath is the great conductor, the body her choir, ruled by air, she gathers her power, and drives the body onward, forward, and we are restored, and grateful to be. We begin again to awaken and soar—any thoughts or feelings of quitting have been simultaneously explored and dismissed. The head grows lighter—so in tune with the breath that the body itself is simultaneously choir and conductor. The instrument finds its rhythm, unleashes its passion, realizes its place in the world.

The body sings a glorious song—legs are alto and arms soprano, belly the tenor, and together they harmonize and build, working together in symphonic perfection. The air is cool and soothing on the skin and clears the nose and throat and mind. There is this clearing and we weigh less because of it and the instrument plays fluidly because it has grown lighter and more efficient. And the eyes don't need to see and the ears don't need to hear and we know beyond the senses what we are experiencing and we move without thinking about movement and we exist without thinking of being, for a moment returning to the source, to a place we forgot we once knew—it feels fantastic yet familiar, enormous yet as light and clear as air.

But we were not meant to sustain this oneness, not yet, not in this physical dimension, this limited maze of space and time. We can glimpse into these moments, but we cannot sustain—for the body is the instrument through which we experience the world, and the instrument will grow dizzy and weary from the journey, and will eventually surrender to itself. And let it surrender with grace, for pride and purpose are no match for the inevitable. The feet grow heavy and the legs begin to give as the weight slowly returns to the awareness and head and spreads itself throughout the body like an expected but unwelcome visitor—taking us by the skin of our neck and dropping us on the doorstep of our life; it must end, for now at least. And we walk away in wonder. And the breeze kisses us gently on the forehead, and reminds us not to forget, and brushes us on the cheek—*Be sure to come back.*

And to know, and not forget, that we can reach these places in the sky without ever leaving the ground—that we can experience truth in such a way—that the road to freedom is endless and paved and lined with earth. That our toes become wings when we forget that they are flesh and bone. That we can travel by foot and touch the sacred, dance with the wind, sing with sky—we've a partner for life, that is life, and life is all we have worth living for.

LAURY KATZ is twenty-five years old and lives in New York City, a city that inspires her every time she walks out the door. This is her first published work.

Fifteen Minutes (of Fame)

Adam Hausman

At the sound of the gun I explode like a sprinter coming out of the blocks, fueled by channeled rebellion and uncorked anxiety. Way out front too fast, I suddenly feel vulnerable and silly for separating myself so awkwardly from the pack. I need to sneak up on this thing, not make myself the target. I drift back as nonchalantly as possible to become one again with the rest of the competition. I must look like an idiot for starting like that at the beginning of a two-mile race. I manage to settle in behind the leader and clear race favorite, Tim Doyle from Fairmont High.

Moments before the start of the race, I had sat with my back against a chain-link fence signing and sealing a contract with myself. Eyes closed, already warmed up and idling, I had a clear vision. I was going to stay with the leaders or die trying. Victory or death, either one would have satisfied me. Any other outcome would have been unacceptable. I saw this. I believed this. I was not new to this approach, this attempted projection of energy. I had tried it before, only to daydream out of my visualizations at the slightest hint of a distraction. Other times I visualized out of my daydreams. I was a confused teenager, lucky just to make it to the starting line on time for the right race and in uniform. That was multitasking. But that night

I was a warrior on a clear path, and my destiny was certain. I don't know what force was present to allow me to act with such conviction. I only know that I had never been able to summon that level of focus and concentration before, nor have I since for that matter.

I'm doing it. I am a major contender in this race. I will not be shaken, stirred but not shaken. It's just hanging on now. Do not let go. That is all I have to do. It is so simple really, just a matter of will. I wish I discovered this earlier. All my other races have been such a waste of time. If he starts his kick right now, I'll follow. If we run so fast I get nauseous I'll puke without breaking stride. What if the pain gets too much? What if I can't make myself suffer? Ah, I've been expecting you, doubt. You're here to sap my desire. But I am a machine built to run, a perfectly efficient running machine. I will not worry, because anxiety equals fatigue. Hell, even these pep talks are tiring. No more thinking. Just run. Run like an animal runs. I allow myself to become lost in the mesh patterns of Doyle's jersey.

I had been experimenting with disassociating myself from the pain, rather than tuning in to it. Of the two methods, it seemed to be the more pleasant technique. It is a form of art to be able to distract oneself like that, and while I was no artist, I was certainly imitating one by trying to make Tim Doyle my muse. Doyle had garnered himself some mystique during the cross-country season by dyeing his hair platinum blond, in a time and community where it was not yet commonplace. He had earned the reputation of being a talented loose cannon, for being just as capable of running a brilliant race as for dropping out with no apparent reason. I remember thinking that *talented loose cannon* was a pretty romantic label to be given. It was much sexier than *consistent middle-of-the-pack guy*, which had come to define me. I feared him the most. "Die trying" would most likely come at his hands, or feet.

I steal a glance back over my shoulder. I know it's not an advised tactic, but I'm very comfortable with my lack of both discipline and restraint. I own those behaviors. No matter, we are all alone. This is really happening! I take a personal inventory and come to the even more shocking realization that I am completely effortless. Don't celebrate yet, best to just find that jersey again. Does a cheetah admire its own speed? No, it just stalks its' prey.

I was not just running for myself that night. Teammates past, graduated seniors back home from conquering collegiate track and field, were there in my corner. I couldn't believe they had bothered to come watch me run in the league championships. They were only a year ahead of me in school, but their wisdom seemed infinite. They had each individually held council with me and pumped me with advice and inspiration. "Stay with that redheaded kid from Beavercreek" had sounded like wartime marching orders. All I really needed to hear, though, I got from Chris Warnock. Now sporting a mohawk and supposedly partying himself right out of his track scholarship, he screamed at me spraying spittle all over my face. "Kick some ass," he said. I basked in his saliva. They were my heart.

Scott and Vineet, my two best friends, were camped at the three-hundred-meter mark of the track. They had each become disillusioned of high school track after some negative experiences with the head track coach, but had come out to support me against their better judgment. Scott, always a head case in the big meets, had never gotten the respect he thought he deserved as a senior last year. He was redeeming himself with some moderate success at the middle-distance events for a small Ohio college. He undoubtedly ran with a seared image of Coach Sommerhill in his brain. He had even coined a phrase. "The best revenge is running well," he had taken to repeating like a mantra. Vineet, a Hindu, had been left off the abbreviated squad for the post-regular-season meets in what he was sure was a racially motivated decision. These two expatriates, isolated from the rest of the scene way over on turn three, were my soul.

Most inspiring of all was Tricia Yates. Consistently running her warm-up laps with me at practice, her attention had completely baffled me. She was beautiful and the defending state champion in the 300-meter hurdles. Why tall, blond, gorgeous, athletic, and smart had any business associating with short, pimply, and goofy I couldn't figure. Success at the league meet meant for an extended season and glorious interaction time with Tricia while preparing for the upcoming district, regional, and state meets. She was my legs.

I'm positively floating. The laps are ticking off, and Doyle is pulling me round and round. I wonder how we could be so far ahead at this pedestrian pace, but the lap splits tell another story. I am running faster than I have ever dreamed. Scott and Vineet look crazed, they're getting more animated every lap. There are no sounds coming from their wildly contorted mouths, though. In fact, the whole place has gone silent. There is just my own steady breathing and the back of Tim Doyle's jersey.

I have heard of this place, but never expected to witness it. I've heard world-class runners speaking of a zone where world records fall. A perfect race run without pain. I'm joyful. I am a joyful boy. Who knew this could be fun? My teammates, I love them. Who else would be my friends? I really love those guys. I love how my brain and body feel after a hard workout. Numb I guess. But the running? Fun? The actual physical act of running? It's torture. This is quite a revelation. I'm torturing myself, every day. Why? Running. To run. It has just been the price to be paid and the sacrifice made. Running has been the price to be paid and the sacrifice made. All my brain and body really need. Run real fast, way out in the lead.

I could not wrap my mind around the idea that I might succeed. But the truth was that I had trained like a maniac. I had been running steadily since the sixth grade, when on a lark I had entered a 5K road race with my dad. I had gotten progressively better each year of high school, but it was still as if becoming a decent runner had snuck up on me. Not only had I been putting together some really decent workouts leading up to this meet, but I was also doing supplemental training at home in my basement. With music blaring and teenage angst seething I jumped rope, lifted weights, and snarled into a mirror. So my parents wouldn't let me watch television on school nights, so be it. Condemned to my underground lair of rage, I did push-ups, sit-ups, stalk around then repeat. The concrete walls were covered with inspirational posters. I had Mike Tyson charging into the center of the ring, bent on destruction. There was the gutsy Steve Prefontaine grimacing in pain, looking beyond the next turn. Always looking ahead beyond the next turn. I wilted them with the moisture of my perspiration. Blindly, I had gotten an edge.

I need to think this through, but rational thought is getting increasingly difficult and alarmingly awkward. What if I break the spell? It's not broke, so maybe I shouldn't try to fix it. Zone out and just keep running. But I can win! Must fight complacency. It would be a shame to have these super-powers and waste them on getting outkicked at the finish line. I have no speed. If he makes the first move, I'm finished. I have to go now.

I pass Doyle with five hundred meters left in the race with the boldest display of outright aggression I have ever mustered in my life. It feels violent. The bell sounds for one lap remaining, and suddenly I hear everything. The noise is deafening and I'm panicking. The bell has exposed me for the imposter that I am, and they're yelling at me. I'm back in a harsh reality where I'm no longer running, more like staggering. For the second time in this race I wonder what kind of idiot I must look like. I cannot stay in the first lane no matter how hard I try. I'm either going to end up in the infield or stray wide across all eight lanes and into all these people. Where have they all come from? All these people wearing hideous looks of morbid desperation. Do they know I'm running in sand?

It turned out Doyle had been rapidly gaining on me. I'd put only twenty meters on him with my initial move, and he'd come within five feet at the end. I collapsed after breaking the tape, more out of habit and a flair for the dramatic than anything else. Scott and Vineet were there first, picking me up. Then they were gone, scurrying away as Coach Sommerhill entered into my still-blurry line of vision. With tears in his eyes, he told me it was the best race he had ever seen run. I melted. I had unknowingly clinched the team title for my school after a tight points race all day long with Doyle's Fairmont High.

I carried myself differently after that. I was an athlete, a runner. I still run. It's mood enhancer, self-medication and meditation time. But inevitably, my mind will wander back to my perfect race. Not a run goes by where I don't replay at least some part of it in my head. It freaks them out on the river trail when I come barreling past right before the parking lot. That day stood for some time as the greatest moment in my life. Well, at least until later that summer when I went on a date with Tricia Yates.

With a keen eye on the future and one foot planted firmly in the "Glory Days," ADAM HAUSMAN teaches high school English in Bend, Oregon. He never won another race.

The Miracle Within

Rob Hamel

No matter how many times I head into the woods, it's the silence, serenity and purity of that which surrounds me that always leaves me breathless before I'm out of breath. I look around and see earth, the real earth. Not concrete, tar, and steel, the side viewed through a smoggy haze. Instead, I find myself privileged enough to see its profile of sod, trees, and streams. My view is bereft of anything unnatural, manufactured, or developed in a lab. It shines without man's ugly handprint, its smell unmarred by his smoky breath. Man couldn't come close to creating something so simultaneously vast yet intimate.

With all that's around me, all to marvel at, my mind wanders. Sure, the beauty of the tall pines and spruce, the majestic mountains in the distance, the subtle whisper of brooks, and the smell of the out-doors never escape my attention. But he who focuses solely on his surroundings is missing more than he sees.

Every so often, on a smooth stretch of trail when it's safe to look somewhere other than at the rocks and roots ten yards ahead of me, with a hint of vanity I'll sneak a peek at my quads. Lines of definition introduce themselves with each stride, then briefly fade away before returning with each step. My legs power me forward, silently. The only sound comes from my shoes plodding over rocks and soil. Never allowing myself but a quick peek, I look up after a handful of strides. Onward I go as my focus moves from the beauty around me to the miracles within me, and then outward again. I take a step, and in that moment an electrical storm reigns. Thanks to the more than forty miles of nerves running through my body, impulses shoot from my brain to muscles through spinal cord, rocketing back and forth at more than 240 miles per hour, moving my every muscle—or so it seems after a particularly hard, long run. My quads and hamstrings and glutes and more contract and relax in the perfect sequence to send me bounding over fallen trees, around rocks, and over soft, forgiving earth. While my personal electrical storm rages, it is silence that prevails—almost.

The wonderful potential stillness and calm is interrupted if I am willing to play close enough attention. My heart, an involuntary muscle over which I have no control, beats at its own pace. It pounds in my chest and I hear and feel its dull, life-giving thud. It echoes at a rate dictated by the most miraculous computer of all, the brain. A mass of gray, spongy tissue with three million miles of axioms is solely responsible for my daily hundred thousand heartbeats and twenty-one thousand breaths. As I run through the wilderness, breathing in the wild around me in long, deep gulps, I sense that Thoreau was right: "The most alive is wildest."

My breathing grows labored. Oxygen is funneled into my lungs. Carbon dioxide is expelled. In this maze of miracles, the trees and plants that surround me each morning, my only reliable company as I pass through the wild, absorb my exhaled waste. My running feeds both the wilderness and my wildness.

There's also the crumble of leaves and twigs beneath my feet, sometimes the grinding of sand, and always the ever-present New Hampshire wind. This wind, with some help from rain and snow, has over the ages worn the White Mountains from Himalayan-sized granite monoliths to piles of rock 6,288 feet tall and less. Given enough time, these mountains will be but a slight rise in the way of some other runner who will traverse these very same paths.

We marvel at the sonic boom of fighter jets, the flash of a meteor as it whisks overhead, or a work of art graced by a gilded frame, all the while overlooking that which happens within us. At times, it's too much to take in. How could I possibly understand it all? I am but a man, a man in a world of miracles, miracles that allow earthen miles to pass beneath my feet and eternal blue to drift overhead. My mind racing, I turn for home, swaying and staggering amid it all. The miles have once again passed by too quickly, thanks mostly to that which I can't control—or fully comprehend.

ROB HAMEL runs, bikes, swims, hikes, teaches high school, and lives in Gorham, New Hampshire, with his wife and three sons.

The Statue of Liberty Wore Nikes

Barbara MacCameron

The Sioux say their world shines when they dance, and I understand that they live for this shining. I get this, not because I have
some expertise on indigenous culture, but because I'm a runner. Well,
a slow-moving woman with extra weight, but shining is grace.
Unearned. After an initial discomfort with inertia, I lose my identity
when I run and become like a monk, a warrior, or a femme fatale.

Run back to New York City with me: 1983, early May, and I've
come to the reservoir. Looking south over forty blocks to the center
of the city, I smell water that has come from the north, and I feel my
strength against Manhattan. The city appears to be child's blocks
with clever spires, an arrangement I might easily topple with a sweep
of my arm. Ducks cruise among weeds adorning the reservoir shore,
more resilient, I think, than Rockefeller Center: ducklings and
weeds. Later I read Hopkins *O let them be left, wildness and wet;/Long
live the weeds and the wilderness yet ("Inversnaid")*.

I veer off the cinder path and am now on a bridle trail beneath a
canopy of blooming cherries. *Blossoms above and blossoms below, St.
Michael, St. Michael wherever I go!* I chant, recognizing the limitations
of my language. *Un Belle Di* and *Siempre Libra* echo across synapses.
Italian arias for running high!

Now it's August and I'm climbing the hill at the north of the park where my breath comes a bit short. Grows a bit wilder up here . . . *New York* magazine reports wolf sightings and sacrificial goats. Suddenly I am under attack as a rock flies past my left eye, and another behind my head. I am not hit, but I am stopped *dead* in my tracks and take cover. I spot my assailants in the woods above the boulders across the road—small children with strong arms. Fear becomes rage as my reptilian brain thunders with blood: I yell to the bikers and runners approaching: *The little bastards are throwing rocks . . . I'm getting a cop.* (I try to sound jaded, but am betrayed by my pronunciation of the word *cop*: I give it three syllables.)

No cop in sight, just the trumpeting angel on St. John the Divine. Bad news up north. I move out again cautiously, anger drying fast into grief. I will never run the north road again. I shorten the park run by taking the east-west cutoff, a bucolic road where, lost in the summer trees, a runner can trick herself into believing she's left the city. Four years later a confident woman will be raped and beaten on my safe road.

The last Sunday in October: No more daylight saving, but strangely humid weather drapes the park in twilight. I walk past a row of ambulances, then through police lines, nearly tripping over exhausted bodies sheathed in glittering thermo blankets. They shiver in spite of the balmy weather. I'm fighting the crowds to the family reunion area where I hope to find my sister. Not enough water on the route today, and no one expected that heat. This may be the aftermath of a recreational event, a thing that people actually elected to do, but in 1985 it feels much more like war. Back then 911 is still a phone number. Yet, there it is: I want to fall on my knees in prayer because everyone has survived.

While I promise my body I will never do this twenty-six-mile thing to it, *ever,* the junkie within coos: *Ooo I can do this, my sister has just finished in four hours.* O, yes, I too could have lain shrouded in silver in some Sunday twilight of late October! I too could witness the demise of my toenails, the blood in my urine. Yippee.

I stick to *fun runs.* New Year's Eve, for instance, in front of the Tavern on the Green: Picture Halloween at the South Pole. It's way past my bedtime, but how often do I get to run through Central Park in the middle of the night? I wear sensible clothing for a bitter night, but I am surrounded by Cabbage Patch Dolls, witches, Raggedy Ann with New Balance, and the Statue of Liberty in Nikes. The couple next to me report they've driven down from Buffalo. Cleverly disguised as the Brooklyn Bridge, with two cabled scarves connecting them, they amorously circle into each other's arms moments before midnight. Hey look, someone observes, *the Brooklyn Bridge is kissing itself!*

This crowd undulates out from the starting line, accompanied by an explosion of color. Like extras from some ur *Toy Story,* we spread ourselves thin in the brittle night. I find my place as the man-made stars die and finish the five amiable miles back to the Tavern on the Green, where champagne is served to us outside. The city encircles the park—hilariously bright, and I tell myself, *I live in New York City, on the cusp of perpetual possibility! Another year, my luck will change!* But my low-tech garb clings to my skin and I fear the nip at my lungs, so I forgo the frivolity and veer northwest at a trot. Into the park. Alone. I glance up at the trees that tower over me and I wonder if some Sanhikan brave had run on this ground one night to keep warm (to warn of terrorists' boats stealing into the Hudson?). *The land you live on,* I tell myself, *is no more, no less than an island in the mouth of a river.* Now I am out of the woods, I keep up the pace as I trot into the city, running in place at the curbsides, gaiety spills from fast cabs. Drive-by hootings! Finally I reach my home, a tiny nest above the Hudson, where I peel off wet things, light the ancient oven, and bake a potato. A pedestrian start to the New York New Year. One of my last there, but I didn't know it at the time.

It's now 2003 and *damn me,* I'm almost sixty! Between two Finger Lakes in western New York, I jog on a long driveway in the wild mornings. My dogs sit under the birch tree; I encourage them to join me but they make a great show of canine disdain lest they should sanction this sham of a walk. Round and round I lumber, breathing in breathing out, stooping each lap to tickle a furry ear. This is another kind of training. Most people walk faster than I jog, but I know that sometime during this ritual, perhaps on the seventh rotation, I'll steal away to that dear country where heart and breath meet. Where shining comes like grace to all-moving bodies. My rational mind, *that dull thing,* perches like a buzzard on the birch . . . it will secure me with its talons when I'm done, nagging me about knee joints, excess weight, faulty parallelism, mixed metaphors and run-on sentences . . . *oh, yeah yeah yeah!*

BARBARA MacCAMERON teaches at the Rochester Institute of Technology. Her interests are environmental literature and Shakespeare.

A New Skin

Sara Lucarelli

It was about one in the morning. I could hear a light rain begin to pitter-pat down from the pregnant clouds above. *There is never anything good on television at this time,* I lamented to myself, sorrowfully stuffing another handful of a generic brand of potato chips in my mouth. A crumb fell out of my jaws onto the remote control. After a brief quarreling within myself whether or not I should brush it off, I decided to leave it be. I changed the channel a time or two. *Hmmm, let's see, an infomercial about a new herb supplement that helps weight loss and also promotes hair growth—or an infomercial about musical oven mitts? Oh, and there was that one about anti-fungus toe spray . . .* I settled on the toe spray, and devoured another handful of chips.

It had been a long, hard day. That's reason enough to veg out, isn't it? Well, in fact, it had been a long hard week . . . and month . . . heck, truth be known, a long hard year. A human is only human and we need some sort of solace to heal us after suffering through a boring job that will never, I have decided, give me a raise, and will never contribute anything to society other than blessing them with my lovely phone voice when they call and I pertly answer *thank you for calling . . . how may I direct your call?* Oh, and I file paperwork, too, so I guess that boosts my importance level a smidge . . .

Besides, any woman who had her heart broken would fall prey to potato chips and infomercials, wouldn't she? Jonathon had promised to love me, forever and ever, and then just . . . just . . . (where's the Kleenex?) . . . just *dumped* me for that pretty little blond veterinarian woman. So what if she helps furry kittens and cute puppies all day and goes home to her quaint little brick house to put on her size 2 dresses and go salsa dancing—which is her hobby, of course—and then on the weekends volunteers at the local Humane Society? She votes at every election, goes to the gym every day . . . Who cares if she is perfect and I am, well, on the other end of the spectrum . . . boo hoo hoo, woe is me. I deserved what I got, I share an apartment with a roommate . . . boo hoo hoo . . . I eat leftover pizza for breakfast . . . boo hoo hooooo . . . I'm ugly . . . I'm terrible . . . I forgot to vote in the last election and ordered Chinese delivery instead . . .

I went to grab another handful of chips, but the bag was empty—not even crumbs left. I threw the bag on the floor. On TV, some perky-breasted girl with shiny long hair was talking about how having foot fungus ruined her love life and her esteem, but *using this spray changed my life! I* threw the remote at her.

"Oh yeah! Foot fungus would be a blessing! You ungrateful cow!" I was shrieking, almost jumping up and down in my seat.

Then I felt the familiar desire to cry swell up like a wave over my body. *I hate myself! I hate my huge thighs, I hate that I am not a cute, animal-loving, healthy, shiny-haired veterinarian! I hate that Jonathon left me! I hate that I know I would leave me if I could!* Then the tears came, echoing the raindrops outside.

The toe fungus infomercial apparently ended—although I didn't remember bemoaning my life that long. A bright garden filled the screen and a handsomely built guy with a muscular, tiny girl came up running through the roses and dandelions, wiping sweat off their faces. As they stopped and began stretching, the girl said in a way-too-happy-voice for someone who was all sweaty, *"Thanks to my new Lightfoot Shoe Soles, calluses, foot pain, and sprains are things of the past!"*

"Yeah" chimed in the man in a meaty I-work-out-voice. *"Now I can keep up with her, no problem!"* She giggles, he smiles, they continue to run, and I decided, sitting under potato chips crumbs, wiping runny lines of mascara off my cheeks, that I was going running. Well, I didn't actually decide to go running, it was more of a thought process like: (1) *I'll show you, infomercial, I can run just as well WITHOUT your stupid shoe soles; and* (2) *Oh God, I think my insides are turning to acid mush-slime from two economy-sized bags of potato chips that are congregating somewhere inside and I need to move around or slip into a cardiac arrest.* Heck, why not? If it worked for these anti-normal, healthy-looking humans, maybe it'd work for lumpy old me. I set about to find my old gym shoes, which were under a forgotten pile of clothes that no longer fit. I dusted them off, swallowed pride before slipping on some spandex pants and a sweatshirt, grabbed my keys, and walked out into the rainy night.

I started out walking a block or two, my hair getting dusted with the sprinkling rain. Ahead was a long stretch of pavement and sidewalk that stretched from this city through to the next, lined with businesses closed for the day. I wondered how on earth I could conquer the massive amount of sidewalk that lay before me. *What am I doing? This is ridiculous; I think shaving my legs is a workout!* But I remembered the happy, chirpy couple on TV and began a slow, even jog, hearing my feet hit the wet sidewalk. I began breathing heavily, seeing my breath before me. Within a block, all I could think about was how badly my legs were beginning to hurt, how my lungs were burning, and how I wished I had Lightfoot Shoe Soles, too.

A block later, I was still managing to keep putting one foot in front of the other. I felt as if my legs had turned to rubber, but something was growing inside me. It was a new, sort of determined feeling. I made up my mind to run to the park, which I knew was a few blocks ahead.

At the next block, the feeling inside had grown a little more—*I was doing it!* Me, who was a moment ago sitting eating potato chips and watching a toe fungus infomercial, was running in the rain and hadn't stopped yet. It was crazy, it was wild, it was sooo urban-modern-healthy! I sort of wished that Jonathon would drive by and think to himself, *Wow, look at her go!* He'd want me back, he'd love me again!

My mind wandered to happy times with Jonathon, having BBQs, making love, laughing over dumb little things. I felt the tears begin to swell up again. I looked down and realized I had begun to run faster.

Another block passed, I was tasting sweat drip into the corner of my mouth. My legs had gone from feeling like rubber to more of a linguini noodle. But I kept going. The feeling inside was spreading all over, a sweet, tingling sensation, and I felt a focus like I never had felt. I had to reach that park, I just *had* to. I wanted to grab it with my hands, pull myself toward it. There were no if ands or buts about it, I was going to reach that park. I focused on each step, telling myself that was one more step behind me. I wanted to give up, wanted to quit . . . I pushed one more step . . . then another, watching as each block flew past me; feeling my mind strip down all the mental blockages that were stored there. That step was my thighs—out of my mind! That step was three months of watching infomercials on Saturday nights! That step was Jonathon—obliterated! Maybe I was just too tired to cry anymore, maybe the pain that was shooting down my flab-in-place-of-muscles was taking over my conscious thoughts.

It didn't matter, I felt free, I had stepped out of my world and into another realm. I felt a burst of energy explode over my body, pushing me forward. I was damp from the rain and my sweat, I was suffering, but I felt suddenly so powerful, so strong. I was reaching a place past pain, a whole new pasture to frolic in.

I reveled in each step, feeling bouncy and light. I breathed the fresh air deep into my lungs. I looked at my reflection in some store's window and smiled back at myself. I had lost a layer of skin a few steps back—felt it slide off my body as a snake sheds its casing, and was now living under a new, vibrant epidermis that hugged me close. The buildings and pavement blurred around me, the world melted away. I kept thinking about each step, and looking forward to the one that would come right afterward. That was all that was vital—all that existed. *I will reach the park! I will reach the park!* I could see it, glistening ahead under the drizzling rain—I could see the slide made of orange plastic, the swings swaying gently in the light breeze. They were my victory—I only had a few more steps to go, a few more steps!

As I reached the sandbox, I slowed down to a jog, and then to a brisk walk. My muscles immediately felt limp. I was drained, but more elated than I had ever been, more satisfied with myself than I thought was possible. I put my head between my knees and caught my breath. I felt a wave come over me, the familiar wave that shook my body every night of the past year. But instead of tears pouring out, I began to laugh.

"*I did it!*" I danced around on my screaming muscles. "*I did it!*"

On the walk home, I felt as though I had never seen the street before, as if I had never seen my reflection in the store window before, as if I'd never walked in the night in the rain before. Well, maybe I hadn't. Nonetheless, the world seemed so fresh, so novel, I wanted to kiss the rain, wanted to embrace the night that surrounded me.

As I approached home, I realized that for a few blocks, I had not thought about Jonathon, about how much I hated my job, how much I hated myself. I had been given a break, and in the absence of these thoughts, I found myself again. I thought I might cry again, but this time, I wouldn't be sad. I was a good person, I was a wonderful person, and I would be happy—I would fix everything about me I didn't like, and learn to love all the things I could not change. I didn't need Jonathon or anyone else to make me feel validated, I didn't need thousands of potato chips to make me feel loved. I wanted to change things. I wanted to feel this way every minute of every day. It was a miracle.

As I crept inside, I saw that I had left the TV on and left the bag of chips lying the floor with crumbs everywhere. It was strange—as if I was watching another life of mine from behind a screen. Before flicking the TV off, I noted that the Lightfoot Soles infomercial had long since ended and another promo was taking its place. I picked up the potato chip bag and swept up the crumbs before hopping into the shower. I knew it was late, and I was feeling exhaustion take over, the adrenaline rush subsiding.

What an epiphany!—the thought struck me that hey, tomorrow would be all right Tomorrow would be great. After work, I would pick up a new pair of running shoes and get an earlier start. Yeah, tomorrow would great. I went to sleep listening to the rain.

SARA LUCARELLI lives in Pasadena, California.

Outrunning My Father

Clara Silverstein

Step, step, inhale. Step, step, exhale.

This is the rhythm that propels me through the year I turn forty-two. My father died when he reached exactly this age. He never ran.

Step, step, inhale. Step, step, exhale.

On my regular morning run through the streets near my Boston home, my feet thump against the pavement. My breath comes in ragged bursts. There's a twinge of pain in my knee, then my ankle. I turn the corner, shed my jacket, and wait for the feeling that usually comes here, about a half mile along: Liftoff.

My father's heart attack was so swift that he kissed me good-bye one March morning, as I left for second grade, and was gone by lunchtime. I walked into a living room full of murmuring adults and the shock that I would never see him again. I was seven years old; my sister, ten. My mother set the tone for our grief: no tears, no hugs, no talking about his abrupt death at all. There were boxes to be packed. Within three months, we moved across the country, back to my mother's hometown of Richmond, Virginia.

My feet continue pounding, but the rest of me is numb. I've risen somewhere above my body. At this level of transcendence, I can best remember my father. First, I see his bald scalp with just a horseshoe of graying hair around the sides, eyes the color of dark-roasted coffee beans, broad shoulders in a plaid shirt. Then I am suffused with the quiet warmth of ordinary days with him. He patiently pushed me as I learned to ride my two-wheeler, his hand firmly under the seat when I wobbled. He sat opposite me at a card table, lining up checkers, pointing out moves that I could take, asking me to choose the best one. As I fell asleep, he perched at the edge of my bed, delighting me again and again with the tale of how he sneaked onto the neighborhood ice wagon when he was a boy. He hid while the wagon kept going. When he finally jumped off, he skinned his knee, started crying, and had to somehow find his way back home.

Growing up without him, my sadness pooled inside of me like stagnant water. I read books far more than I talked. My studies kept me churning forward through high school and college. If I let myself stop and look too far down, I thought I would drown in all the tears I had never cried.

I didn't start running until the year I turned forty. By then, I had settled in Boston with my husband and two children. It took reaching midlife to make me reconsider the benefits of running. I had always admired the joggers who pounded past me, but every attempt I made to join them left me doubled over with a stitch in my side. I stayed in shape by biking, swimming laps, and taking long walks. My father's weight was normal, but he never exercised much; maybe it could have saved his life. I worried that a gene for heart disease was hiding deep within my cells, waiting for its chance to strike. I feared repeating the family history, one day suddenly keeling over, vanishing from my husband and children. I became determined to fight back, to strengthen my heart, to outrun the father who died young, and to trample my feelings of my own vulnerability.

I survived my earliest runs with more determination than ability.

Just five minutes left me exhausted and gasping. I gave myself a month to keep trying. To my surprise, my stamina improved little by little. I actually began to look forward to losing myself in the rhythm of my feet and my breath. As I felt healthier, I felt more confident that I would not be doomed to the same untimely death as my father.

Step, step, inhale. Step, step, exhale.

During the morning run, I imagine my father cheering me as I slog up the hill that is nicknamed "Heartbreak" by the Boston Marathoners. On other days, I imagine reaching up to take his hand, skipping to keep up with his gait, just as I did when I was a girl. On still others, I picture him waiting for me at the end of a trail, which gently curves so the end is never visible, weeping willow branches like fireworks overhead. Sometimes, my mind is far beyond my father, skating across the sky—a surface without boundaries, where I can glide and just keep gliding beyond the constraints of time.

At the crest of Heartbreak Hill, I sweep past the crowns of oak and maple trees, the slate rooftops of Victorian homes, the squirrels skittering along the electric wires. Far below, my body plods along. Soon, it will ask me for a sip of water or a walk break. I'll have to go back down to rejoin it, turn around and head home.

I have slowly worked my way up to completing a 5K, a 10K, a half-marathon, a marathon. I'm training now to finish my second marathon. With every step, every mile, I am strengthening myself to outrun the number of years that my father had to live. Yet with every mile, I am also closer to finding out that he has never really left me. The tears that I never cried have vaporized, trailing behind me like a fine and rainbowed mist.

Step, step, inhale. Step, step, exhale . . .

CLARA SILVERSTEIN, a writer and editor at the *Boston Herald,* is a published poet and author of the memoir *White Girl: A Story of School Desegregation* (University of Georgia Press, 2004). A mother of two, she began running in 2000, the year she turned forty, and completed her first marathon in dead last place!

A Run with My Father

Leonard Topolski

It has been almost eight years now since one of the most significant events in my life crossed paths with my love of running, forever melding the two into a powerful memory that still comes back to me this day as if it just happened. I will always look upon this day as a confirmation of my faith in God, as well as a sign that running for me will always be more than just a recreational endeavor.

The day was perfect for another long run that would provide the training necessary for an upcoming marathon, as well as a distraction from the stress of a family tragedy that was unfolding in my life. A group of friends and myself got together to run loops around the San Jacinto Monument, site of a great limestone obelisk that marked the most important location in the history of Texas independence. It was a course we were comfortably familiar with, providing a quiet place to train and reflect upon the history of the area. It was never lost on me that such a battlefield provided us a chance to express our own sense of freedom.

The weeks preceding this early-December day were filled with an event that rushed toward inevitability, despite my desire to somehow control its outcome to my own ending. For years my father had fought a slowly ravaging battle with the effects of diabetes melitis. At first it was just the acceptance of a radical lifetime change in diet and a daily litany of injections. Inevitably it became a subtle failure of his circulatory system that led to a loss of hearing in one ear and blood flow to his legs, which had taken away his love of the game of golf. All of this contributed to ebbing of his will to live, despite my pleadings. My last conversation with him as he again entered the hospital was with a man who had a sound of defeat in his voice.

Running was my escape. While I could not forget the great changes that were occurring, I could at least escape them for a short time each day. The distance I traveled that day was a great as the one that lay between Texas and my father in New York. I tried to rationally cling to the hope that he would again leave the hospital to pursue more time on earth, but I knew in my heart that his days were limited.

I ran the first few miles with my group, but my distractions and need for an emotional release carried me faster than they were able to maintain, and probably beyond what my own body needed to train. I felt a great detachment that day from my own physical limitations, allowing myself to be controlled by forces I could little understand. The air was crisp and the sky was a brilliant blue, as the sun rose up to greet another early-winter day. It was somewhere during the final quarter of the five-mile loop that an event occurred that I can only explain as being the intervention of a force I will never understand. It was as if the sky suddenly opened up and I felt transported, only momentarily, to a place free of pain and frustration.

I no longer felt the earth passing beneath my feet, nor was I aware of even my own breathing. There was a distinct feeling of nirvana that the uninitiated might credit to a runner's high; but I had experienced that in the past and knew that this was something completely different. The feeling was an almost overwhelming sense of being omnipotent, except this was during a training run where I was not running at a particularly taxing pace.

At the time I did not have the ability to understand what had happened to me, only to marvel at how good it made me feel. The run was perfect that morning, made even more so by some seeming intervention of a higher being. I felt a greater peace than I had in weeks, and rushed home to share it with the one person in the world I knew could understand it.

A hesitant nurse answered the phone in the hospital and told me my mother had headed back home. I assumed this was temporary, since she had spent the past few weeks living with my father at the hospital during his treatment. I asked the nurse how he was doing, only to be curtly told that he was doing better. The response surprised me only in its tone of useless information, which I credited to a person who seemed to be doing her job with a lack of compassion. It was only later when I reached my mother that I found out why the nurse had actually been reluctant to share the bad news with me. It was then that I realized that his time of passing exactly correlated to the surreal moment that had occurred while I was out on my run. I don't consider myself to be a deeply religious person, but this day will always remain in my mind as one where I felt the spirit of my father depart the earth, finally free of the pain that had filled his last days.

LEONARD TOPOLSKI is a forty-three-year-old father of two, living and running in Pearland, Texas. He is employed in the petrochemical industry. He has been running for over twenty years and is most proud of having completed the Houston Marathon nineteen years in a row. When not running, he enjoys reading, gardening, and writing the newsletter for his running club, as well as articles for local running publications.

Running to Him

Shelley Ann Wake

The dream was always the same. I was always running. Running out of the house, and over a fence, and across a yard, and onto the street, and down the highway, and across the land, and onto the beach. Running so fast that my feet meet the water and stay on the water and I am running across the ocean. My feet send up little sprays of white as I run across the blue water. I see the green of islands as a blur as I keep running.

And as I see the island that holds him rising up on the horizon, I see him. He's running across the ocean toward me. I stop. He stops. The water gives way beneath us as we fall into the ocean. I try to swim toward him but the ocean sweeps me back toward the shore. I reach my hand up to wave and I see him do the same. And then he is gone as we are both swept away back to our own shores.

I wake in my bed, alone. I think of his hand reaching out and how close we were. But I don't feel longing or loss. I just feel complete relief that he is all right. He is an ocean away but he is all right. He is not with me, but he is somewhere. That's all that matters for now.

My husband had been away for just a week when the dreams started. The night before he left I received a call. He had been given the orders and he was off to East Timor, off to fight a war, off to save a nation of innocent people. There was no time to ask questions. No time to ask how long he'd be gone for, or what he'd be doing, or if he'd be safe, or if he'd be back. There was only time to say, "I love you, see you soon." See you soon. Three simple words I've said a thousand times. But this time they weren't just words. They were a prayer. So I said that, hung up the phone, and tried to get on with my life. I didn't even know he'd arrived until I saw it on the news. I didn't receive a call to say he'd arrived safely. I didn't know anything except that he was over there somewhere.

And after a week, the dreams started. Always running. Always running so quickly that the miles melt away and I see him reaching for me. See him enough to know that he is all right, not enough to know anything else. I sit up in bed and let the relief flood over me. For twenty-three hours and fifty-five minutes of the day, the thought that he might not be all right floats in the back of my mind. For five minutes, I sit in bed and feel in my heart that he is all right. But then the real thoughts surface again. *It's just a dream. It's just wishful thinking. It doesn't mean anything. But it does*, I plead with myself, *it does mean something. I feel it. I feel it. I feel he's all right.* I don't want it to, but the real world always floats back. The fear enters my mind again as I lay down and try to sleep. I never can. Instead, I lie there as the sun comes up trying to convince myself that he's all right.

After seven days of waking from the dream, one morning I did something new. I got out of bed, I got dressed, and I went running. I didn't run to the beach, and I didn't run across the ocean. I just ran through the streets and kept on running. And somewhere at the point where the body wants to stop running, it happened. The pain in the legs was forgotten, the thoughts in my mind were forgotten. I was immersed in my running and the only thing I was aware of was the rhythm of my footsteps pounding in time to the beat of my heart.

And as I reach that point where I can't hear my thoughts anymore, I know. I know without thinking that he's all right. Without logic, without thought, without doubt, I just know. And at that point, I stop, I turn around, and I walk home, ready to get on with the day.

After two weeks of my running routine I returned home one morning and found a letter waiting in the letterbox.

"I can't stop thinking about you and I pray you're all right," he wrote. "I keep having these dreams that I'm running toward you. But of course, I'm not. I'm just running around the base every morning because our instructor makes us. You know I hate running and I hate mornings, but it's actually become the best part of my day. Somehow when I'm running, I sort of feel that you're all right, if that makes any sense."

It made perfect sense to me.

SHELLEY ANN WAKE is a full-time author, poet, and essayist. Her work has been published in various magazines, e-zines, and anthologies in Australia, Great Britain, Canada, and the United States. She is currently completing a masters in professional writing, and working on her second collection of short fiction. She lives in Australia.

Conversation with a New Running Partner

Kay Sexton

"There should be an acronym for women like me, LADIEs perhaps: Late At Developing Interest in Exercise. There's no excuse, but I didn't run until I was thirty-nine years old. And I never had a runner's high. Second wind, yes. That amazing feeling when you realize you've just run your first mile, or for your first hour, or your first ten miles, yes—but never a runner's high. I'm a ten-minute miler by and large, and ten miles is as far as I want to run, thank you. But my plodding miles mean as much to me as Paula Radcliffe's swift ones do to her, and I do it without the endorphin-kicking, turbo-boosting, barrier-blasting runner's high. Dare I say it? Yeah, I dare. Maybe it's a girl thing? Some have one every time, some have one only if the conditions are perfect, and some enjoy the process without ever having one at all. That was my theory anyway. And it remains true, although over the past year I've learned to run an eight-minute mile and I hope one day to be able to run two of them consecutively! And I could run a half-marathon now, if I wanted to, which I don't, and I call myself a runner even if I'm injured, or I haven't run for a couple of weeks, which I never would have dared to do a few months ago. A runner without a high—like a rebel without a cause? Well, almost.

"You see, there was this one time, at Bexhill. My first 10K. But before I tell the story, you have to put yourself in my shoes—literally. Size five or thirty-nine, my second-ever pair of Brooks Illusions (ladies). You have to be 1.65 meters tall, thirty-nine years old, female, and running your third-ever race and your first-ever 10K. Got it? Probably not, but never mind, you'll be as close as it's humanly possible to be—runners are the world's best at knowing how it feels to walk a mile in somebody else's shoes—you've only got to look at another runner, limping, striding, smashing records, or sweating fountains, to know just how he or she feels. That's part of why we do it, right?

"I chose Bexhill because the entry form said 'flat and fast,' but when I got there, I discovered that I hadn't read it carefully enough: 'flat and fast' came below the 5K race date and above the 10K one, so you had a fifty-fifty chance of applying it to the right race. Guess who got it wrong?

"It wasn't flat—there was a huge hill. It wasn't out and back either, but a three-lap course, which meant that hill had to be beaten three times. Fast? Well, allowing for the hill, and it being the hottest day of the year, it might be a fast race, for the lucky ones.

"It's a funny thing that you can be hotter than the Sahara at noon but your hands can be icy. Five minutes before the race starts and I'm shaking my hands to try and get some feeling back into them. Cold hands, jumping heart, lack of concentration, gut clenching like a fist: Why do we put ourselves through this? Those last five minutes are the worst I have ever lived: worse than childbirth, much worse than driving tests or exams, incomparably worse than having a tattoo or visiting the dentist. Tell me again why we do this? My race number seems to be weighing me down and the heat is draining my energy away—I envy the men who are running in string vests. My hands are still numb and cold, though.

"The start is, as they always are, a horrible mess—I go wrong-foot first, stumble, and take an elbow in the chest from a runner ahead of me. I watch the field stream away like a reverse comet, like I'm standing still and they're all running, but—dammit—I'm running as hard as I can! Then, settling down, finding my own pace—okay: my own plod—and getting on with it. The hill is the turnaround point. You run up it, halfway down the other side to the water station, turnaround and run back to the crown and then down again. To add to the fun, runners on the first half of the lap get to do a little off-road work on a grassy, duney bit of wasteland, so that runners starting the second half of the lap get to hare down the hill on the road without crashing into anybody coming the other way. So we've got an uphill, a downhill, a water station, an uphill and a downhill. And when I say hill, I am talking typical British understatement here: This thing is steep!

"There is a heat-haze belly-dancing across the road as I approach the hill for the first time. Most of the field is already streaming (and steaming) back down, on my left. The hill looks like a great wave about to break its tarmacadam crest over me. I know I will never beat it three times. Once maybe, twice with luck, three times never, so I decide to give it all I've got, on the basis that caution is useless.

"There's a guy ahead of me, midthirties, not a club runner, puffing and grunting. Can I overtake him on the hill? Yes. Easily. So easily in fact that I stop running after a couple of seconds to look back and make sure he's okay. He is. He's also behind me. I have just overtaken my first runner.

"From the top of the hill, we look like a kid's necklace. I can see bright figures pretty evenly spaced around the whole course. It's lovely. And hard work. And I manage one half of one sip of water before spilling all the rest. Less pondering, more running!

"Second lap and the hill looms at me as soon as I turn around. I have become metronomic and although I know the danger I can't stop myself counting steps—it will slow me down, that's what all the running books say—but on the slog that is the approach to hell-hill, I welcome anything that keeps me moving, slow or fast. If I can complete two laps then I think I can retire, without disgrace. The hill jiggles in front of me again, wobbling around like gray jelly on a seaside plate. Runners coming toward me are attenuated and wavering, like underwater aliens. They're fast, though: As each one passes me, I hear panting breath and fast footsteps. There is no breeze until the crown of the hill, so I hook my motivation to the fugitive gust of air that will reward me when I make it to the top. There's a guy ahead of me, club vest, shaking sweat from his hair as he thumps his way up. Can I? Well . . . if I dig deep, shorten my stride, get up on my toes and . . .

"There is nobody between me and the hilltop.

"I don't know where he went. I don't know where I went! The next thing I'm clear about is that I'm running the downhill, with a plastic cup in my hand that I cannot remember taking. Either he vanished or I overtook him. Wow! I dump the contents of the cup roughly in the direction of my mouth and I fly down that hill. Cold water bounces off my hair and shoulders, and something has happened in my veins. That phrase 'the blood singing in your ears'—I never knew what it meant until now. Normally blood thumps in mine, in diastolic/systolic rhythms that remind me how hard I'm working. But now, my blood is serenading me on two high clear notes, ah-ah, ah-ah, or perhaps it's not my blood—perhaps there's a violinist nearby, or maybe the crowd has begun to chant wordlessly? Stupid—it's definitely coming from me. And it's so loud that I can't hear my feet pounding the road. In fact, when I look down, they aren't pounding, my knees are lifting, my arms are engaged, and I'm simply soaring. I have one thought only, *This must be a runner's high!*

"As I complete my second lap I hear the roar that salutes the winner coming home. It's Freddie T'sjoen, coming home like a bullet with a bandana, and I feel sudden, totally rational awe that I train on the same track as the man who has won this race. I am so happy for him that I'm almost crying. And I'm so happy for me that I'm singing a little nonsense song to myself and I head along the flat to the hill, and the gym teacher in my head is telling me to slow down because it will all end in tears, I'll never be able to keep this up. I'm singing 'I don't care what people say—I'm going to run this race my way' under my breath and grinning at every runner and spectator I see. I grin at the hill and don't ever bother to think about it, if there's anybody ahead of me, then they'd better give track: Me and this hill have got a thing going!

"The sun, sparkling on the sea, is no longer a harsh distraction from the race. I look over and admire the rhinestone wavelets and hear the harsh cries of the gulls. I trust my body to carry on this race without my direction, and I am free to appreciate the gorgeous day and enjoy the heat that is bouncing and slamming off the promenade and bringing a huge crowd of holidaymakers to watch us as we run. The sounds of waves, cheers, seagulls, and other runners make a wonderful syncopation to the refrain of my blood. I think, *There cannot be anything better than this.* And I am wrong. At the top of the hill, a clean, light breeze lifts my hair and washes my face with coolness— I look down at all the other runners, some finished and cooling down, others steaming for their personal-best times, and some behind even me and toiling to catch me—that was the best moment, ever. We were all part of this human chain, making our best efforts, achieving what is possible, and sometimes being surprised in the process. There are no words to explain how it feels . . .

"It didn't last of course. By the time I completed lap three and made it across the finish line, my arms ached as though I'd run the whole distance cradling an oil drum and my legs had that indescribable feeling of being at once as heavy as telegraph poles yet as weak as ice cream melting in the sun. I was so tired my eyes kept closing in midstride.

"That was last summer. Like with childbirth, I have forgotten the pain and discomfort, but I only have to hear somebody say *Bexhill* and I can remember the sound of my blood singing in my veins. Runner's high—rarer than rubies and brighter than diamonds—every woman should have at least one."

Kay Sexton spent two years as an agony aunt for nudists—it was an education, although for what is not clear. She is also a philosophy graduate, recreational runner, and hostage to a capricious muse. She is a Jerry Jazz Fiction Award winner, with a quarterly column at www.moon dance.org. Her website http://www.charybdis.freeserve.co.uk gives details of her current and forthcoming publications.

Milestone

Melissa Garrison Elliott

I was raised as a fundamentalist Christian. A basic tenet of fundamentalism is that this world is not our home. We are here on our way to somewhere else. This world is a vale of tears and a trial by fire, a test of our ability to cling to God and turn away from evil. Our reward will be to leave this mortal coil and proceed to heaven, where our real, true existence will begin at long last.

If the world is not our home, neither are our bodies. Though we refrained from drinking and smoking, I never got the message that this was to keep our bodies healthy to do God's work; rather, it was the abstention from the evil encountered in connection with these activities. We weren't allowed to dance, either, which bore out this theory. Dancing is good exercise for the body, but in the mind of the fundamentalist, dancing leads to illicit behavior (translation: sex) and was therefore to be shunned regardless of its cardiovascular benefits.

I grew up with the belief that my body was a suitcase for my soul, ultimately unimportant in the greater scheme of attaining my reward in heaven. As a result, I felt ill at ease with and within my physical self—never quite grounded, not often present. When I was a child, I was the last or next-to-last chubby, clumsy candidate chosen for the baseball team. I couldn't hit, couldn't throw, couldn't run. As I grew taller and began to acquire a womanly shape, I dieted religiously to keep my weight within twenty pounds of the supermodels I idolized on the pages of *Seventeen* magazine, but never really had a sense of myself as a physical being, an earthly creature.

I went away to college at seventeen and promptly lost fifteen pounds from making the long walk from the main campus to my dormitory at least four times a day. But after a while, eating high-carb cafeteria fare (and taking frequent trips down to town for a Baskin Robbins double cone) took its toll, and the pounds started to pile on.

At Pepperdine University, a college founded by a member of the Church of Christ and still closely tied into the church teachings in 1977, we were required to take two religion classes as part of our undergraduate curriculum. With a few exceptions, they were not taught by rigid fundamentalists but by some of the most forward-thinking and ecumenically oriented of my Christian brethren. From them I discovered that much of what I had been taught as a fundamentalist was fundamentally wrong. I found out that the Church of Christ was not founded by Peter and Paul in first-century Jerusalem, but by Thomas and Alexander Campbell in the seventeenth-century Midwest. I found out that the King James Bible (the deity actually worshiped by the Church of Christ) was not dictated word for word by God to the apostles but was assembled and edited down from a much greater body of work by the Council of Nicea in A.D. 325, and that it was and remains the most inaccurate translation of the Bible ever made. I drank knowledge like holy communion, and knowledge became my new religion as faith in the old, small, rigid one faded away.

Since my early years of failure at all team sports known to P.E. teachers, I had avoided physical activity. But now, as I became grounded in this world by looking critically at the next, I longed to excel at something real, tangible, and, most of all, mindless. All the philosophizing was giving me a headache, and all the sitting was giving me secretary spread. My dormitory, one of the three farthest from the main campus, overlooked the college track, where herds of boys in training for various sports pounded out their daily miles. One day while browsing through the library stacks on a break from studying, I came across a book called *Running for Health and Beauty: A Complete Guide for Women,* by Kathryn Lance. The cover said "Running can help you lose weight, sleep better, improve your complexion, increase your energy, even change the way you feel about your life." With those pairs of pounding feet in my mind's eye, I checked out the book.

The following weekend, I made the trip over the canyon to the closest shopping mall and bought my first pair of running shoes. On Monday, dressed in sweatpants and T-shirt, I headed for the track at 5 P.M., a low-traffic time when most students were cafeteria-bound for dinner. I had never done this before; I didn't want to humiliate myself. My caution paid off. I staggered to a breathless halt after jogging slowly around less than half the track. The track was a quarter mile; how sad was I? But I remembered the woman who wrote the book, who couldn't make it halfway down her block when she started, and I persevered. I jogged till I ran out of breath, then walked, then jogged, then walked, until I completed two circuits of the track—half a mile. I retired to my dorm, exhausted but satisfied, and returned at 5 P.M. the following day.

Jog by jog, the distance crept upward. The first high point came when I made it around the track once without stopping to pant. I allowed myself to enjoy that distance for a week, then started trying to add to it. Slowly, by sixteenth-mile increments, my distance increased. Finally, one day two months later, I found myself on the last long side of the oval on the fourth lap and decided to go for it. Accelerating from my usual jog, I clenched my fists, ducked my head, and pumped my lead-filled legs as if they were well-oiled pistons, and finished the mile in style.

When my heart rate returned to normal, I danced up the stairs to the road and up the sidewalk to my dorm, grinning from ear to ear. In the lobby was a group of guys waiting for their girlfriends to come down and walk with them to dinner. These were the five black girls who lived in Suite E at the top of my dorm, they and their boyfriends the only black people in the entire mismatched Wonder Bread bunch of redneck fundamentalists and surfer dudes and chicks that populated Pepperdine. I liked them.

"What are you grinning about?" one of the boyfriends asked me as I dashed through the door and headed to my room.

I struck a pose, hand on one hip, and announced, "I just ran a mile!"

"So?" one of the others said.

"So?! So I just ran the first mile of my life!" I answered.

"Good for you," the first guy said, frowning at his friend. "You keep that up, now."

"I will," I said, and headed for the shower.

As I turned the corner to my suite, I heard him say, "That girl has the best ass on a white woman I ever saw." With the memory of obnoxious construction workers yelling, "Hey, Bubble Butt!" running through my mind, I grinned wider. For the first time in my life, I had been complimented for my physical appearance without feeling embarrassed or uncomfortable. I had run a mile in this body. It was my body, and I had the power to affect it. That day it quit being a suitcase and became my true home.

MELISSA GARRISON ELLIOTT is a movie title designer, a Sunday painter, and a writer of articles, essays, and stories. She has been published in the knitting anthology *The Threads That Bind,* and in *Veggie Life* magazine, *The Downtown News,* and *The Advocate.* She has lived in Los Angeles for thirty years.

Soaring Over the Wall

Andrew F. Martin

I have always been somewhat of a skeptic when it comes to Eastern religions. I don't find golden statues of obese Buddhas, yogis breathing themselves into contortions, or gurus ministering to the wallets of their assembled flocks particularly inspiring. I do, however, admit to having a dangerously limited knowledge on the subject.

My understanding of the concepts of meditation, reincarnation and the search for one's inner Karma is superficial, and extends little beyond the popular Western interpretation. However, one can't help wondering if these religions do in fact hold some mysterious secret key, that elusive "something more" that can show the path to providing a deeper meaning to one's life. Little did I realize that the eighteen-mile mark of my first marathon race in 1994 would give me a chance to find out.

My family had decided that my decision to run a marathon was the most ridiculous thing they had ever heard. I remember my wife's words. "You must be mad. You're forty-one years old. Take a look at yourself in the mirror for God's sake. Isn't it time you let go of some of these teenage fantasies?" But that didn't stop me from committing myself to a grueling training schedule, with its lonely hours of self-imposed agony. Fulfillment of my dream had its price: aching limbs, uncounted frigid miles through snow and sleet, whatever it took to feed my madness. What made me do it? I don't know. Perhaps running was my Karma, and I couldn't resist the call.

At the start of the race I was excited. Ready and eager with limbs full of vigor. I had never done the distance before, but I trusted my training. Somehow, I knew in my soul that I could finish. This was a chance to show my abilities to a disbelieving world.

The first half of the race was relatively uneventful, a pleasant run through the picturesque streets of Victoria, British Columbia. The inner harbor with its blue water, sailboats and fishermen mingling on the piers, and a gentle early-morning breeze rustling through the oak trees lining the wide boulevards made a perfect backdrop for the race.

Initially, I chatted with the other runners as I ran, and marveled at the ever-changing kaleidoscope of humanity surrounding me. Martha from Courtenay was doing her ninth marathon, her wiry body poking out of oversized crimson shorts. Bob from Vancouver was having no trouble keeping up with me, still doing marathons at the age of sixty-seven, with a twinkle in his eyes behind his bushy gray beard.

But now the sun was high in the sky, mercilessly baking the pavement and the runners below. My pace was slowing. My initial early-morning yin of nervous energy had turned into a rhythmic yang of sweat and dedication. As it progressed I paid less attention to the other runners, and just like a yogi in meditation, I started saving my energy by concentrating on my breathing. I was barely aware of the other runners, let alone where they were from or the color of their clothes.

The relentless dusty miles were taking their toll. The excitement, enthusiasm, and bravado had long since evaporated, leaving behind nothing but aching limbs and a stoic determination to continue, to prove to the world that I could finish what I'd started. I was going to make it to the finish line.

Just eight miles to go, I told myself. All I had to do was stay focused and keep going to complete a lifelong dream of finishing a marathon. I could already visualize crossing the finish line, the final strides of the race, the cheering crowds, the flash of cameras, and the admiration of my peers. And that's when I hit the Wall.

The Wall is not made of bricks and mortar, but any marathon runner can attest that it feels just as real. It is that defining moment, like a precipice at the end of the road to exhaustion, when your body knows you just can't go on. Every drop of energy has been drained from every limb. When your body runs out of steam, there is nothing left to give. No amount of mental effort will save you from having to stop.

I knew, in a general sense, from my trainer to be wary of the Wall, but I hadn't prepared myself for anything like this. I had no idea that the Wall could be this sudden and this daunting. Based on how hard I had hit it, I knew that for me the race was over. My efforts had been futile. I had failed. In a grueling marathon race you either have the combination of ability and training to overcome the Wall, or you don't. I did not.

I staggered as a wave of nausea engulfed me. Scarcely aware of my surroundings I made a superhuman effort to take one more step, but even that was little more than a stumble. I just couldn't go on.

But even as I stumbled, my mantra, the little voice inside me that I'd become so used to hearing during my training, was keeping up its steady rhythm. *Stay focused—Don't stop—You can do it—Only eight miles to go—Stay focused—Don't stop* . . . My limbs were refusing to cooperate, but my mind kept right on going. *Stay focused—Don't stop—You can do it—Only eight miles to go.*

But this was survival, not meditation. Mentally I knew I had to concentrate on my breathing or I would collapse from exhaustion. I had no choice but to change the tune in my head. *Breathe in—breathe out—Stay focused (stumble)—breathe in—breathe out—Don't stop (stumble)—breathe in—breathe out—You can do it.*

As I stumbled, I synchronized my feeble steps to the new mantra. My mind repeated the words in an endless tune. Stumbling plods had replaced paces, near oblivion replaced consciousness—but at least I sensed that I was still moving.

The individual faces in the sea of smiling supporters were nothing more than a blur in a blob of faceless humanity. Their shouts of encouragement were close to inaudible; all I could focus on was the mantra in my head.

"There he is, Mom!" I heard my nine-year-old daughter Michelle yell from the crowd. My mind struggled to focus and to separate her face from the crowd, but it was just too much energy. I was grateful for her support, but my body was too exhausted to care.

Perhaps I was passing some near-death experience, my brain starved of oxygen. Or maybe it was an endorphin-induced high triggered by my running. But, at that moment, I felt an all-enveloping white light wash over me. Was this death from exhaustion? Oblivion? Nirvana?

But despite what was happening, my mantra kept going with its relentless little tune. *Breathe in—breathe out—Stay focused—breathe in—breathe out—Don't stop.*

My body somehow answered the call, gradually achieving a new state of awareness and peace. This was something that I can't find words to describe, a sensation that I had never experienced before. Somehow I was free, and my mortal body was irrelevant. I was over the Wall and my spirit soared. I completed the last eight miles in a dreamlike trance.

So, was it some sort of transcendence to a higher state of consciousness? Was it an inner awakening or a religious experience? Perhaps the white light was God, or the Holy Spirit, enveloping my soul. I came away from the experience with as many questions as answers.

But the one answer, of which I am sure, is that for me to have done what I did, there was definitely "something more." It cannot be categorized or explained, only experienced at a deeply personal level. It just "is". There is no other explanation for how I overcame that Wall. To understand, you need to experience it for yourself.

I believe that I know why I had this experience. It was to open my mind to my soul, and to teach me a lesson about walls. It also allowed me to set a new goal (although I still haven't had the courage to tell my wife). It's a goal for how I'm going to spend my sixtieth birthday.

My lesson was: No wall can contain the human spirit. No matter how thick and how tall the structure, no matter how strong the mortar, or how massive the blocks, with persistence every wall will tumble down, sometimes one tiny chip at a time.

The same applies to the challenges of our daily lives, whether emotional or physical. We may, at times, have to rely on forces that we do not know we have, and things we do not even understand. But with persistence, training, and the right attitude, few goals are truly impossible. After every challenge, there is also an opportunity to set a new goal, a little more challenging than the first.

By running the Victoria Marathon in October 1994, I found out about the "something more" in my life. Now it is your turn to challenge yourself, run that race, swim that stream, or climb that mountain. You, too, can learn how to overcome walls and soar.

Oh, by the way, did I mention my next wall? Ever heard of Mount Everest?

ANDREW MARTIN works as an electrical engineer in British Columbia, Canada. He enjoys a variety of outdoor activities such as running. Andrew is proud of completing the Victoria Marathon but considers it merely a milestone on the road to even greater achievements.

Fireflies

Heidi E. Johnson

I remember myself, a small child with short dark hair and freckles that bloom over my summer cheeks like dandelion fields. I'm sporting a white T-shirt with Mickey and Minnie smooching in a frame of pink heart, the words LOVE IS in bold black under their feet. Brown corduroy swishes between my legs as I chase after fireflies in a darkening field that paws at my narrow chest.

Three other kids accompany me, our elbows bearing the tickling blades as we crush neighboring stalks beneath our sneaker-clad feet in an effort to add to the blinking mass in our jars. Our voices are hushed, our breath deep and jagged. Every limb and layer of tissue exults in the hunt, bending and pouncing in every direction to procure the delectable vision of captured light.

It was a complete feeling, as if every molecule that bonds together in the formation of my body was activated, rubbed, massaged into life, like I was dipped into god serum, infused with the same light that illuminated my blinking prisoners.

Years later sitting on my cat-tattered couch, tendrils of smoke flowing gracefully from my nose, the "freshman fifteen" hanging dutifully from my flanks, I remembered the wild abandon of my firefly days. Somewhere deep down inside my depressed mind, where my parents dangled from the tree of childhood blame and my self-esteem floated in a bilge bucket I had helped to create but could not destroy, I remembered that my limbs were not meant to feel leaden and my heart was not meant to beat a drum cadence toward death. The child chasing fireflies had somehow gotten herself caught in the glass jar and I longed to twist the cap to let her out.

I slid on my walking sneakers, white canvas Nikes with bright red shoelaces pulling together age-worn uppers, and stretched my confused limbs for the first time since high school track. To my dismay, my knee, which used to meet my forehead with ease, bobbed six inches below the uneven ridge of my uncut bangs.

Out on the road, I put one foot in front of the other, moving forward slowly at first, then more quickly as I warmed up. It felt good to be moving, like I was making a change, scratching off old skin. After half a mile, however, a dull pain reached up my shins like the multi-veined cleavage of an earthquake. I willed it away, maliciously biting into the graveled side of the road with each revolving heel.

There is a rhythm you can get into when you're running, a rhythm I remembered from high school but couldn't reproduce on that long hot road, wearing bulky shorts that rubbed between my thighs, underwear that floated downward in an uncomfortable mass between my legs, and a heavy cotton T-shirt that suffocated me in the cruel heat of midafternoon.

The pain in my shins became sharper with every step, piercing my concentration and begging me to stop and walk. When I did, I could feel and hear my heartbeat in my chest as beads of stinging sweat emptied into the corners of my eyes. I turned around and stared down the road, waves of heat vapor distorting my depth perception, hoping I had made it at least a mile and knowing I had not.

My mouth ringed with dry foam, I began the long walk home, discouraged and angry. Was I in enough pain to be walking or had I become too fat and lazy to finish a couple of miles? I avoided the answer to that question for over two years, though it nagged at me persistently in quiet times.

I began with shorter runs, pushing myself a little farther and then a little farther still, until I had pushed my daily runs up to five or six miles and my long runs to eight or ten. My body felt energized. My limbs felt light and agile, primed for movement. Every fiber in my body felt healthy and strong, as it hadn't for years. The cap had been twisted and I fluttered out, eyes blinking eagerly at the new freedoms allowed me.

Winter's breath had formed ribbons of crystal that lined the road to town. My week-old Bowerman-series sneakers crunched a crisp rhythm against the grainy pavement. Each muscle in my foot moved with precision, rolling in perfect alignment from heel to toe, working with powerful calf muscles to propel me gracefully forward. I was a machine, well lubricated and ostensibly indestructible, ready for the demands of the eleven-mile run I had undertaken for the morning.

I would finally do it, break the ten-mile barrier, and I could feel my blood speeding around its veined racetrack, jubilantly anticipating an endorphin-doused adventure. I focused on the road ahead, certain that every human, swishing by at fifty miles an hour in their comfy vehicle, knew that I was running eleven miles and suffered a small stroke of jealousy over my vitality. My posture was linear, my arms swung loosely, I felt aerodynamic enough to fly.

The road was flat but well ornamented. At about one mile, I passed Rick's, where five wooden canoes poked their ends from a dirt-flecked snowbank, like dolphins bursting from the foam of a wave. Another mile brought me to a farm that leaned sharply down into a mud- and manure-dotted hill. I thought how uncomfortable it must be to conduct the business of a farm on such steep ground. Nearly every house along the road puffed soft clouds of smoke from its chimney, creating the incongruous scent of a campfire in the frigid air.

My energy was strong through the sixth mile, carrying me as effortlessly as a father shouldering an infant. But somewhere near the beginning of the seventh mile, my body began to admit some exhaustion, its complaints building slowly through the mile until I could no longer ignore its vociferous pleading.

My chest collapsed ever so slightly and I realized that I was still two miles from stopping and that two miles of walking was not an option in fifteen-degree weather. Out of excitement, I had run the first six miles at a much brisker pace than usual. It felt as if a leak had sprung in my legs and arms and my energy was pouring out onto the ground in a thin stream from my joints.

I tried to keep up my speed but my limbs were useless, so back to my yoga roots I went, like a wayward Christian searching out God in hard times. I focused the small amount of energy I had on putting one foot in front of the other and raising and lowering my diaphragm to circulate more oxygen through my lungs. I continued in this way, my pace slowing by at least a minute per mile, forcing my chest out when cars passed so that nobody would discover my exhaustion.

For the last mile I was in a trance. I knew the contours of the road more completely than those of my own face. So many times had I run over the hills and sprinted the flats, dodging on and off the pavement depending on the quality of the shoulder. I surfed upon these details, allowing them to carry me past the iced-over beaver pond, around the snow pile of Ballou's that the town never plowed because he kept his old beast of a Ford parked there, and finally down the long twisting driveway to the snowbank that acted as my finish line.

I bent down toward the snowbank with an urgent thirst that

threatened to toss me to the ground. Half a mile separated me from my home, making snow my only immediate thirst-quenching option. My stomach twisted inside me, punishing me for overusing its delicate tissues. I grabbed a handful of questionable snow and crunched slowly on its crystals, leaning on a birch for support.

My initial feelings of defeat dissipated quickly as I realized I had reached the end. I made my way triumphantly home, each step reminding me of my accomplishment. It had been such a long road to get there, but there I was and I felt as though I were lifting off, soaring up, up, and away, a firefly outwitting the sneaking children with their deceptively transparent jars.

HEIDI JOHNSON is a freelance writer and an avid runner. She lives in Vermont with her husband and daughter.

Maybe Tomorrow

Abigail A. Crago

As I stepped outside into the shadow of the morning, my lungs began to waken, though my body was slow to follow suit. The grass was peppered with beads of dew, and the air hung like a wet blanket over my shoulders. A soft fog deepened the darkness of the early morning, and the pale moon did little to lighten the earth. My head began to dizzy with activities as I thought of all the tasks ahead of me that day. "Not now," I scolded. I relaxed my body, shook out my arms, and closed my eyes. I let my body fall limp from my waist and felt the sore muscles in my legs stretching to just beyond comfort. I continued to stretch, feeling the toned muscles throughout my body gradually wakening. From the top of the driveway where I was standing, I could barely see the end, but I knew exactly what awaited me in the darkness.

Taking one last deep breath, I started my trot. The mechanical sound of my watch starting was lost in the chorus of the summer morning. Chirping crickets, humming grasshoppers, and singing birds all gave natural rhythm to my pace. There was no horizon to lead me or light to guide me; all that directed me was the familiarity of my daily course and my innate drive to persevere. My breath was steady, not yet labored. As my muscles loosened, my legs instinctively began to lengthen their stride. Gravel crunched beneath my feet, and the rocks pressed through my worn Nikes on the fresh tar-and-chip road. The tar smell rose to my nose and mixed with the scent of the warm wet grass.

Behind, I could feel the sun's light beginning to chase me, but darkness still lay in front of me. Not even halfway through my run and already my pace had more than doubled. I glided over the empty road as if my legs were made of air rather than flesh and bone. My lungs were full of the fresh air, but they were light, and my head was empty of any preoccupations. My eyes narrowed and focused on the nebulous road laid out before me. Miles of road, in the middle of God's country, paved for me to conquer. My legs lifted higher to my chest, and my arms swung freely at my side. It was bliss to run in the cover of the early morning, to be the closest human to all of natural creation.

The sun continued to rise, and I could no longer outrun the rays. I felt the light hit my back, and its warmth intensified my own body heat. Sweat was pouring down my arms, my face, even my legs. I loved the taste of the salty sweat as it ran from my forehead to my lips. The sweet bitterness pushed me onward. I wanted more. I wanted to run until there was no more paved way to take, until I could find my own trail to blaze.

My legs weren't heavy on the pavement, my lungs weren't desperate for air, my head was free from all distraction. My heart was beating in unison with God's. I could feel Him breathing for me, through me. His air was my air, His strength became my strength, and when I came upon the wall too high to climb, He lifted me up to set me gently on the other side.

Back in the driveway, stretching for the finish line, my watch was audible when it stopped. The day had begun, the world was spinning, and creation had gone back to hiding. I had seen the world as God sees it—as pristine, perfect, and made for me. I stood in the driveway; my breath was heavier than it had been while I was running. My legs began to burn with exhaustion and tremble with heaviness. My mind was clouded with feelings of pain, ache, and fatigue.

A smile was creeping on my face. Joy was sneaking into my soul. Peace was smothering my conscience. I had just run the fastest three miles of my career. No one had made me rise before the sun. The sheer passion and anticipation had roused me from my slumber, until I could no longer lie in bed imagining, I had to run. The sun was peeking over the horizon, melting away the dew and the fog. The darkness was now fading; the stars gave way to red and orange streaks, the moon forfeiting its reign to the sun. I hadn't beaten the sun, but maybe tomorrow. I couldn't wait for tomorrow.

ABIGAIL CRAGO is nineteen years old and a student at Gardner-Webb University, where she runs cross-country and track.

My Daily Tranquility

Leslie Cave

I approached my fifth mile panting, my breath becoming erratic. It was one of those hot, dry midsummer days when the sun's relentless heat attempts to discourage one's steadfast determination. The urge to stop was immense, but I was halfway to finishing my ten-mile daily run and it would be pointless to walk five miles back. I focused on each breath, inhaling and exhaling slowly to gain composure. With my sudden concentration I noticed the developing picture in the sky. The fluffy clouds in front of me were shaped like small sailboats roughly painted on a vivid blue backdrop. I was visually captured, yet my feet still ran forward at their normal pace. Droplets of water pooled on my skin. My mind raced around each cloud, noticing all the unique details. One cloud's shape in particular reminded me of the time I went sailing while on vacation in Maine. I suddenly felt the overwhelming calmness of sailing on the ocean; the salty air filling my senses, the wind whipping against the back of my neck. The sun glistened on my skin and I could feel the burning sensation on my face. I listened to the rippling sound of the moving water around me, while in the background I could hear the intermittent gulps of nearby fish nibbling bits of air just above the water's edge.

A high-pitched car horn startled me and I was awakened from my reminiscence. I was no longer sailing, but running on the small dreary gray path. Instead of salty air, I was surrounded by fumes from the cars speeding by to my left. I looked over my shoulder to see where the disruption came from and my heart regained its steady beat. I felt the strain on my legs and the air moving quickly in my lungs. How far had I run? I noticed the empty field up ahead with its sporadic patches of burned-out grass that told a story of the sun's travel, and realized I had just run another mile. The feeling of calmness disappeared and I yearned to finish my route. I felt my leg muscles pound against the hard concrete road and the rolling pebble in my shoe consistently make an impression in the ball of my foot. The moisture became a suffocating layer over my skin and my head throbbed from the heat. I heard my voice speak silently with encouraging words as I unwillingly continued on. To my right, I noticed a mother with her infant walking in the park. The baby's carriage wheels squeaked in a timely pattern, creating a mesmerizing sound that was in sync with my pace.

At that moment my heart slowed and I imagined holding the baby in my own arms; its soft skin and tiny hands in mine. I visualized the baby's placid blue eyes looking up at me with pure dependence. My body relaxed and my breathing was once again calm. The piercing cry of the infant carried my imagination to when I was in my mother's arms, which by thought alone gave me an overwhelming feeling of warmth. I heard my mother's soothing words and smelled the comforting scent of my favorite baby blanket. Her laugh echoed in my ears and I smiled as I thought of her.

This time my daydreaming was interrupted by my sudden cough. My head ached from the sun's pounding heat, and my hair withered under my cap. I could feel my cardiovascular system working hard and my heart getting stronger with every beat. I envisioned what my heart looked like and thought of all the images of hearts I had seen, both real and symbolic. I thought of how the heart became a depiction of love and soon my exploring mind traveled to my first love. He was tall, dark, and ever so smart; I was young, pretty, and ever so naïve. My heart melted as if it were just yesterday, yet it continued to beat steadily as my feet continued running on their path.

Before I knew it, I came upon the dilapidated red barn to alert me that I was nearing the ten-mile mark. I felt the exhilaration of finishing my daily run and making better time than yesterday. I glanced at the flowering trees, the brilliant blue sky, and the many distinctive houses that lined the road. As I gazed at these things, I realized that each day as I run, I'm taken on another fulfilling journey in my mind. Running makes my thought process clear, sharp, and ready to face life's challenges and obstacles. I'm more observant and have the ability to relax and control my breathing, staying calm and aware throughout the day. My body feels refreshed and I feel alive.

As I slowed down to a fast walk, I wiped the perspiration off my brow and took off my soggy cap. I relinquished my head to the sun's heat and my damp hair quickly dried. My eyes squinted to the blazing glare and I took one last breath before I was brought back to my reality.

LESLIE CAVE lives north of Boston, Massachusetts. She is married and has two lovable Basenji dogs. As a marketing professional, her hobbies include writing, running, and spending time with her family.

How Humans Fly

Dan Sturn

More than our friends who think we're crazy, or our doctors and mothers warning about shin splints, or our spouses wishing we'd spend the time with them, we runners wonder why we run. We wonder this when the alarm clock rings, sending our mind into a shiver of *not yet, not yet.* We wonder this on the cold morning pavement.

I wondered this from day one, when I asked myself again and again: *Why am I doing this?* At that time, I only wanted to start and finish. That's all. Just start. And then just finish.

Soon I started logging distance, as if my worth could be improved by how far I ran before letting myself collapse. And my self-image did improve, as did my appearance, which started fifty pounds overweight.

I quickly learned to bury my problems in my "at-least-I-can-run" mantra.

"I may come home late from work, but at least I can run a mile a day," I'd say.

Or, "Sorry I'm not into your new-age group, but at least I can run 1.4 miles a day."

And: "Hey, I might be a bad husband who forgets his wife's birthday and then makes it worse by running to the grocery store for flowers, but at least I can run the 1.6 miles to that grocery store."

Which led to: "So you're gonna blow ninety dollars a week on counseling. At least I can run 2.3 miles," I'd yell, then add, "for free!"

And then finally, "Go ahead and leave, dammit! I can use the extra time to break three miles."

She had no clue why I kept my equipment by the bed: running shorts, pedometer, portable CD player, and sports watch. Of course, the core essentials . . . thick white socks and running shoes . . . waited by the door, along with my chosen shirt for the morning.

And then I'd be off.

Listening to my heavy feet awkwardly slap slap slap, I'd put one foot in front of the other anyway, and by the third deci-mile I'd be envisioning muscles, tan and firm, complementing my flat belly and healthy heart. And when that vision no longer worked I would answer that nagging why-do-this by stating over and over the "mere" distance between me and my goal.

"Only a mere 0.6 mile," I would whisper between gasps, feeling how much my lungs wanted to burst out of my chest, how much my heavy arms and stiff shoulders ached, how my feet and knees felt like Silly Putty. While I looked down at the pavement, my mind witnessed determination quarreling incessantly with awareness—

—but then I learned to take that awareness away.

The Art of Distraction turned this wake-up ritual into a sport about scenery and CDs. And thanks to the distractions, the constant and bizarre aches and pains eventually surrendered to wandering thoughts and worries.

"Damn her new-age counselor," I'd whisper between pants. "I'm not going. She should grow up, forget this high school touchy-feely crap."

Huff, puff, huff, puff.

"Life is about willpower, about racing against the next guy, and I'm winning that race, dammit! For her! I'm making good money."

And after a few more strides I'd pant, "I'll bet that running trail at the bottom of her counselor's multiplex is a twenty-miler."

I still kept track of the "mere-ness," greeting each deci-mile as if it had its own personality, ever stressing the end, that to make it through the "mere" distance would reward me with honor and worth.

Yes, worth! Still the answer to "why run?" I slowly worked my way to a twelve-minute mile, down to twenty-five pounds overweight, now seeking health rather than appearance. But occasionally I would find myself taking one long deep breath through several strides, then returning to the standard huff and puff. And sometimes I'd discover gaps between my internal dialogue, which grew wider and wider as I continued to run.

For two years the Art of Distraction furthered my conscious decision to reach my potential. I whittled down to ten pounds overweight, going to the Boston Marathon website and dreaming, *What if I was worth that much?*

When my wife and I brawled, I would sneak out of the house to run. She called this running away. But I thought I knew why I ran: the independence, the physical health, the mental stamina, the adrenaline, the worth!

And just when I thought I understood why I ran, she left me.

She informed me during a cold spring thunderstorm, while I languished on the basement treadmill, irritated that she had turned the television off, muttering "fat chance in hell" in response to her reminding me of the one last counseling session tomorrow morning, purposely scheduled to start after my morning jog. "If you really love me," she had said with suitcase in hand, "you'll be there."

I found a new answer to "why I run" that next morning, on mile seven of a twelve-miler. During a tempo that helped me pump through my anger, I suddenly realized my distractions had disappeared.

This wasn't just a gap. My CD player must have dropped somewhere, and I didn't recognize the scenery, or the teens sneaking home from a night of partying. I must have been lost.

Then I noticed my feet silently gliding over the pavement, like a poet's pen across the page. I felt my arms swinging easily at my side, like I was swimming or . . . or . . .

Flying?

My feet left the ground. They continued their gait, and I realized that I was . . . yes! Flying!

My arms no longer pumped; they propelled. I flew through a weightless world as a perfectly designed machine, coasting up hills and dancing across fields. Colors had no hierarchy: the red trees and purple lawns and yellow roads and sparkly white cars all held the same brilliance.

I held my hands out like wings and sailed down a hill. I tasted salt on my lips, and realized tears streamed down my cheeks.

I flew closer and closer to the place mystics and shamans and acidheads all try to describe. Each moment became precious. I felt simultaneously all alone and completely connected, at one with the pavement that led to an unknown destiny, lost in a chanting breath, the in and out of it moving me forward, to the point where time slipped by fluently as the ground passed beneath my feet.

I later wondered if I had endured an out-of-body experience, standing at a finish line, watching myself run. And while I watched I saw that I ran totally alone, not only down there, running down the pavement, but throughout my life, as a whole.

And though this new understanding left me feeling lonely, I didn't fight it. Instead I invited it to run with me, and it appeared, as a wingless angel. She flickered out in front of me, wearing super-bright-white running shorts, shoes, and shirt. I ran up alongside her, and we flew down a hill together.

She held her white-gloved finger to her lips, inviting me to listen to the wind rushing past me, to the crickets and the water in the creek and the breeze weaving its way through the leaves in the trees that I passed, beyond the buzz in my head that's always there, and the ringing behind that buzz, and the fluttering of her feet. She flew beside me, addressing me with a familiar smile, and then suddenly she darted off ahead of me, and I propelled faster to keep up with her, chasing her over a bridge and around a barn and back under the same bridge and just as I caught up to her, she swung around, facing me, flying backward, and I realized she was *her*! My wife!

My God! I had been chasing my wife. She smiled, then flitted ahead at least twenty paces and kept that distance as I tried to catch her.

Then she was gone in a flash of sparkles, leaving me alone again. I continued to fly, thinking that like it or not, nothing is guaranteed except the fact that nothing is guaranteed. I came into this world alone and I'll leave it alone. But my true worth revealed itself. And that worth had nothing to do with how far I could run.

I flew higher, up a hill, recognizing my neighborhood, pulling the loneliness with me, until another revelation struck: I didn't need her to understand me. I needed to understand *her*!

And I came crashing into my driveway, dragging my five-pound-below-ideal-weight body to the porch, breathing: "My God! My God! My God!"

My worth wasn't based on accomplishments. It was my capacity to share my self, my real self, my love.

Love for my wife.

When I finally stopped at my doorstep, leaning on the porch column while allowing my breath to idle down, my thoughts returned to a normal pace.

"I love her," I said between breaths. "I love her."

I quickly untied my shoes, trying to catch up to the day. My thoughts raced to that counseling session.

Once there I sat in the lobby, reflecting that I had connected the earth to the sky through me, the real me, the me who no longer tracks distance, the me who looks out the window and sees that trail winding around the city, not as a twenty-miler but as a trail to be explored, as a container for my next meditation.

And as I contemplate this trail, I realize there's power in running. Real power. The power to inspire, the power to connect with, the power to run toward and not from. The power to figure out who you are and why you are precious. The power to love.

So now I run that trail every day, on the way to our session together, and I run it to catch up with my mind and pass it, until I feel as light and spacious as the sky, until I'm flying, alongside God Himself, loving my time alone with Him, flying through the trail, no longer feeling my body, loving my body for its ability to propel me through time and space, watching the trail go by, until the final mile sneaks up and disappoints me. My sports watch no longer measures worth, but tells me if I have enough time to stay a little longer on the trail, so I can stay with my God and my Self, and increase my capacity to love.

Like a monk meditates merely for meditation, I run because I run, to increase my capacity for compassion, to tap into my ability to love. Because running is meditation. But loving . . . that's how humans fly.

DAN STURN writes in and about central Indiana, where he lives with his wife, Stacey Hadaway, and their two children, Dani and Jacki.

Feed Your Head

Katherine Montalto

The cold gray sky folded in around me. I took a deep breath as I stepped onto the path through the park. My pupils dilated to the size of small pinheads as they adjusted to bright sun shining through the dull clouds. This was to be my first run, the first time I had done any real physical activity.

The last four years of my life had been spent in a blur of psychodelic drug use. At first I felt like I had been expanding my mind and consciousness. It seemed the only way to have fun. If I was having trouble organizing my thoughts around something, this was a way for me to get them back in line. I felt like it pushed me to think beyond myself and into the world and how things worked within it. Eventually it became tired and predictable, no longer pushing me beyond my limits. It only held me in a state of suspended animation, making me numb to the things I once cared about.

I had only quit just before high school graduation. There in the park of that following winter I took my first run. Since quitting I was having a trouble finding ways to occupy my time. I couldn't maintain any focus. I needed a new way to attain free-flowing unhindered thought, but in a constructive way. One I could remember the next day.

I started slow at first, really just walking. Then into a slow and steady jog. I took in a breath of cold winter air. It was crisp and clean. Like a knife, it cut away all the damage and disease of my lungs. My slow dull blood began to run hot and at a steady pace. Even though I couldn't see it, I felt as though I could feel it change from black to red. The cold stiff wind against my face quickly eroded away all the damage I had piled on in the last four years. I began to pick up the pace and move in to a slow but sedulous run. My unstable mind was eased into a lull by the combined rhythms of my feet hitting the pavement, the pulse of my heart pounding from my chest into my ears and by the sound of the hot breath I could see reaching in and out of my mouth. The clarity this rhythm provided felt like water rinsing my mind. My blood rushed to the surface of my skin to keep me warm and I began to feel elated. A tingling started from the top of my head, worked its way down over my face and into my chest. It reached my belly warm and soothing moving down into my legs and then my feet. My vision became very crisp and clear. Colors seemed brighter. Everything was seen with such detail that it almost looked too real, like it had been painted. I looked at my surroundings carefully. The snow on the ground seemed so white that it was glowing. The leaves on the trees had long been dead, yet there still seemed to be so much life behind each naked branch I could almost hear their breath as it whispered across the back of my neck.

The running high has a lot of the same physical traits as a drug-induced high, but is still very different. My mind is clear enough to stop thinking about myself but to think of the world and how things work within it. It doesn't leave me full of self-doubt afterward. I begin to feel tired and sore, but fed with every step instead of drained like after a night of doing drugs. With drugs the intensity is unpredictable. It comes about without warning. With the first run I felt myself build up to it and was very in control. I could keep up the same pace and enjoy, or I could push myself farther. With drugs it is intense at first then fades out. It is hollow gratification, an empty-calorie experience, and I was always left feeling spent. At the end of the first run the high had peaked with the satisfaction of knowing I had accomplished something. I had found a way to organize my thoughts and expand my mind in a productive way that didn't damage me physically.

I use running now to clear the clutter of my mind. It helps me to enjoy the solitude I crave. Instead of watching TV or doing drugs, to try to catch a moment alone with myself, I run. With running I'm using my solitude instead of being in solitude.

Before this first run in the park I had tried working out at a gym. It always felt so unfulfilling, running in place while watching TV. It seemed more about achieving some superficial unachievable goal, so-called perfection, an artificial ideal. Running outside in the winter alone felt so much deeper than that. It was about bringing back the spirituality of physical activity. I realized how interconnected the spiritual, emotional, and physical parts of me were. They work together always. If one is neglected the health of the others suffers.

KATHERINE MONTALTO lives in Chicago.

The Ocean High

Pam Gershkoff

There's nothing like the fresh ocean air. The waves pounding on the shore as my heart pounds in my chest. The surf crashes, the white foam rushes to cover the sand, as my feet rush to cover more and more of the pavement. I'm invigorated by the wind blowing through my hair as my eyes scan the vista. Here and there, a dolphin breaks through the water; a seagull swoops down to cool its feathers in the chill of the Pacific Ocean.

There's something about running next to the ocean that is unlike any other experience. I happen to live in California now, but I grew up on the East Coast and felt the same exuberance there.

The sounds and smells of the ocean propel me forward as I run. I am lost in my thoughts, as though in a trance. The busy world of cars, congestion, and business is left behind. Although there are always other people around, they don't intrude on my time or space. There is an etiquette to running that quickly becomes apparent. Sometimes I have to move left or right to let someone by or to pass a fellow runner going at a slower pace. We each have our own rhythm that moves us forward, as one foot follows the other in rapid succession. But we never stop to chat; that would invade the privacy of the moment. That would disturb the tempo. Silence is part of the runners' unwritten code.

I'm in a vacuum where only I exist. I can think about whatever I want to—real or imaginary. Occasionally, clouds emerge, trying to distract me with their formations that look like animals or figures. I'm totally mesmerized by the view, by the experience. All of my senses are on high alert.

I try to count my steps, but they come far too rapidly. I check my watch to see how much farther until I reach my goal. Like a mirage, the destination keeps eluding me until, lost in my thoughts, I realize that I'm almost there. Maybe the appeal of running on the beach is that I can be anyone I want to be; maybe it's that I can escape to any-where. My only constraint is my imagination, which tends to work overtime, fueled by the sight, smells, and sounds around me.

I try to think about the things I have to accomplish when I return home, but my mind is a blank stretching to eternity like the ocean off to my side. I can't have a serious conversation with myself because I'm in an abyss of tranquility. Momentarily, I think about my family and how my morning run is not just for me, but for them, so I can live a healthy, long life and be around for those I love. Maybe that's just my excuse that keeps me from feeling guilty about taking time out for myself. Maybe that's my justification of why this is the best part of my day. I probably should say that the best time is spent with family and friends; but being outdoors, I'm refueling every inch of my being— inside and outside. I can't duplicate the feeling any other way. I truly get an "ocean high" from the experience.

One of the added benefits about running is that it costs absolutely nothing except my time. Time can never be recaptured, but how can I use my time any better than running by the beach? The strands of sun stream down, glistening on the water. I am the artist re-creating this scene in my mind. I think about the various shades of blue, green, and purple that comprise the ocean. I watch as the waves break on the sand. How much of what I see is lost on most people who just run, staring down at the bland pavement below their feet? I think about the picture I will paint when I return home, but somehow the scene is all forgotten when I walk through the door. Like a fog it dissipates. The phone is ringing; the e-mails are waiting on the computer; the meetings are scheduled. I feel trapped; my house becomes a cage that keeps me inside. I'm back to the "real" world of deadlines and commitments. My whole body tenses up, as I realize that I can't relax and dream until tomorrow. I'm not free again until the morning when I'm back running by the water, lured by the sounds and smells that are calling me.

PAM GERSHKOFF is a freelance writer in southern California. Her articles have been published in numerous newspapers and magazines, including the *Arlington Star-Telegram, Dallas Morning News, Reform Judaism,* and *Positive Parenting.* She coauthored *The Select Sorority,* a play about former first ladies that has been performed frequently by the Palos Verdes Peninsula Branch of the American Association of University Women.

Sunrise, the Desert, and Five Thousand Years of History

Tracy Musacchio

I am already awake at 5:15 A.M. when my alarm rings. The call to prayer, echoing from a local minaret, woke me about an hour earlier. Now it's finally time to get out of bed.

I push the mosquito net aside, assess the night's flea bite damage, and climb out of bed. I put on my running shoes and a T-shirt and, as a concession to the conservative Muslim culture, an ankle-length skirt. Not my favorite outfit for a run, but I've been in Egypt for a few months and I'm adapting to the idiosyncrasies. I've begun to like the way the material feels swishing around my ankles. In the distance, I hear the clanging of a man banging a wrench against a propane tank, making his fuel-selling business available to anyone who happens to stop his donkey cart. In this part of Egypt, the Arabic word for "propane tank" doubles as slang for a chubby person. Sometimes, when they see me running, our Egyptian workmen point and joke, telling me in Arabic to get going so that I don't become a propane tank. That keeps me running, as does my love for the hearty Egyptian food that we eat.

As I leave my room, I see the archaeologists piling into the cab for their daily trek down to the site of our project. My duty is not to dig, but to stay behind in order to record and draw the objects that the archaeologists find. They start working immediately with the sunrise (to maximize their daylight hours) while we in the house start work at a more leisurely 6:30 A.M. This gives me the chance to get in an early-morning run before the afternoon sun gets too dangerous. It's barely comfortable already at this hour of the morning, probably around 80 degrees. The temperature will quickly rise to about 115 degrees before the middle of the day. We work until the heat becomes unbearable, around 2 P.M. Then we squeeze in a few more work hours in the evening as the sun is setting. It makes for a long day, but in the desert, there are few distractions.

The sun is rising as I leave our house for my run. Although miles of sandy desert stretch out invitingly in one direction and in another direction is a quaint and open village, I run in laps around our house to keep the guards at ease. Our house is guarded twenty-four hours a day by the Egyptian tourist police. This province has been suspected as a seat of terrorism, so the guards are required to keep constant and protective track of all foreigners. Their watch duty includes following us on foot if we leave the house. Prior to September 11, 2001, the guards were a mildly inconvenient but necessary annoyance; now, looking back, I am grateful for the consideration of the Egyptian government. The guards don't look exactly ready to chase me, in their black wool suits and their combat boots with their large machine guns. There is a likely broken but still menacing tank parked near our house (to protect us, although it is aimed at us), and I certainly do not want my run to necessitate its use. So I run in circles around the house.

Usually the guards are not bothered by my running—actually, they are amused by it. Most days, my run will prompt them to lift weights in a show of masculine bravado that transcends cultural barriers. They wave hello at me, asking me how I am. The appropriate Arabic response is "*tammam, insha'allah.*" "Fine, God willing." Nothing is certain in Egypt; everything is at God's will.

And I leave my run to God's will. I have always enjoyed running, through multiple marathons, freezing cold winters, hot and humid summers, seven apartments in four cities, and two stress fractures. Being in Egypt has taken my love of running to a new level. Even during my best runs at home, day-to-day trivialities are ever-present. Here, there is no sense of the day-to-day. Running becomes simply the joy: of seeing the great expanse of desert and the sunrise; the village with small huts and children walking cows and water buffalo; the five-thousand-year old Shunet el-Zebib (the funerary temple for an ancient king and the oldest architectural structure still standing); the cliffs rising above the desert floor, marking riverbeds that dried thousands of years before. The scarab beetles that scurry across the desert sand, pushing their balls of dung. The Egyptian women in brightly colored dresses tending their fields, vivid even across the desert, hastily and sheepishly covering themselves with long black scarves when they see non-family-members. The feeling of having nothing on your mind except for exactly the sensations you are experiencing. The beauty. The pleasure of life. The joy of living.

I run selfishly, for myself, with no regard for time or distance but simply for enjoyment. The only words I can possibly think of to describe the experience come off as cliché: overwhelming, majestic, awe inspiring, breathtaking, stunning. My run is leisurely at points, hard at points. I see the same desert that the ancient Egyptians saw and I can't help but think of the Egyptians who were here before; I can't help but think of the continual flow of time and my own insignificant part in it.

I've promised some friends that next February I will run in the Egyptian marathon. Hopefully I'll record my first top-ten-female finish there (typically, only about ten females complete the full marathon). While I'm looking forward to it, that experience won't be nearly as personal. During the marathon, I will be thinking about pacing, hydration, and seeing my friends waiting for me at certain mile markers; not beauty, stillness, the meaning of life, and the mystery of life.

In a few days, I will board the train for the nine-hour train ride north from our site of Abydos to Cairo. After that, I will fly from Cairo to JFK International Airport in New York—an abrupt awakening to American culture, and a rough way to end my trip to Egypt. But Egypt is a lot like running: Once you've truly experienced it, once it is inside of you and it takes control of you, you can't resist it. I know that I will return to Egypt and I know that I will continue running. *Insha'allah.*

TRACY MUSACCHIO is a Ph.D. student in Egyptian language studying Egyptology at the University of Pennsylvania. Running is the only indulgence she currently allows herself, with dissertation research consuming most of her time.

Something That Happens

Stephanie Hawkins

If five years ago someone had told me that there was such thing as a "runner's high" I would have thought they were crazy or trying to sell me running shoes. As a beginning runner, I could barely last two minutes at a steady jog without gasping for air and crying about my entire body hurting. I was convinced at only twenty-one years old that I would never be a runner. Some people just don't have it, right? Well, something inside of me couldn't let that be the end of it. Runners are amazing. They have beautiful bodies and healthy outlooks on life and activity and I was determined to find out how to achieve those same elements. I took one step at a time, gradually increasing my intervals, and before I knew it running was my drug of choice.

Obviously running is not easy. If it were, everyone would be superbly fit and the corner coffee shop would be obsolete. It takes time. Rarely can anyone strap on running shoes and begin a euphoric run within seconds. For most, there is that "warm-up" period when you may wish you were somewhere else, anywhere else, or that the half hour would just be over already! However, once you begrudgingly force your way through the first segment of your run (for me it is usually about five minutes), something incredible happens. No longer are you clawing your way out of your cardio but rather clinging to the moments you have left. Breathing becomes clearer and more rhythmic. Thoughts become more pleasant and positive. Your footsteps pounding on the surface below you become cadenced, and your body suddenly feels alive! Could this be it? Could this be the seemingly fictional rumor I've heard along? Yes, I believe it is; it has to be. This, self, is the runner's high.

Amazingly, the discomfort that once consumed my body is gone. My legs that once ached now seem to be invisible. I can't stop. I want to go faster. My chest is clear and filled with fresh air and my breathing seems to tingle my nose like a medicinal dose. I look for visual markers along my journey where before I would allow myself to screech to a walk, only now I surpass them wondering why I underestimated my ability. Sunshine appears to be vibrant yellow, casting a delicious glow on my surroundings. The people and things I pass I can't help but to smile at, for life is good! Nothing seems angry or unpleasant or sad or hassled. Perhaps the whole world feels my euphoria! I think. Maybe not, but my perception of the hurried life around me is sugarcoated at this moment and that is okay with me. Life is too short, I think. Too many things are taken for granted, I think. The tribulations of my daily routine suddenly seem easily conquerable, or at least tolerable, and I am eager to face the challenges that lie before me.

As I continue on my journey, I take in the serenity around me. The breeze among the trees is peaceful. The faraway traffic that usually sounds so urban and foul suddenly becomes lulling white noise, like a fan blowing on a hot summer day. I feel the perspiration trickling down my neck and chest, tickling my skin, when I realize that my time alone to gather my thoughts is coming to an abrupt end. I begin to slow my pace and absorb the refreshment I feel. The tingling sensation in my body reminds me why I love this experience and I embrace it. My entire day is better, my mood enhanced, and I feel healthy. Not even magic coffee could take me this far.

My next mission is to pass the gossip along. Being a fitness trainer by profession, it is my duty to assist others in the process of weight loss and achieving an overall healthy lifestyle. But it can't stop there, at least not for me. I, personally, do not like to force my way through a workout, nor do I expect my clients to do so. I encourage exercising to be fun and something to look forward to, although it isn't always so easy.

One client, a forty-something woman who really needs a push in the motivation department, usually starts her routine workout with a desperate plea to stick to light walking. I oblige . . . sort of. We start with a walk to warm up and gradually increase the speed until she is at a brisk pace. I then inform her that we are just going to add twenty- to thirty-second intervals of light jogging, to which she begrudgingly agrees. The first few intervals are challenging but before long she is requesting a few more than instructed. Her reason? "There's just something that happens when I'm running that makes me not want to stop," she says. I smile, for my real mission for the day has been accomplished. "That," I happily tell her, "is what we like to call the runner's high."

STEPHANIE HAWKINS is a twenty-six-year-old former fitness trainer in Destin, Florida. She is currently an at-home mom with a three-month-old . . . and still running.

Running to Agnostos

John A. Cantrill

The preacher has me singing about the friend I have in Jesus as the warmth flows over the revival meeting. Burdens are lifted from my heart. Always a practical thinker, I have trouble coming to the same conclusions, but the crowd and the girls and the rhythm and the rhyming all have their effect on my young heart. I give in to the religious sirens luring me to their houses of worship. I am born again.

There is comfort in spiritual thinking. A sense of purpose and meaning is given to life. It must be attractive, for so many fall under its spell. Only the bottle rivals it for adherents, but I could never get too close to the suds without physical unhappiness. So I plod along with the word of God and the community of believers, always a bit out of step but nevertheless in line.

And many years later, I am in line again, running the Marine Corps marathon with that same crowd of unknowns, only less dressed. The girls are still sweet but tougher. I am part of this wave of people as my feet find their predestined beat. The hours of training sing to me like angels from heaven. I am alive and very well and oh so sure of my quest. As the minutes pass and the murmuring of the masses fades, I find myself filled with the Holy Spirit. A calm peacefulness comes over me, which can only be likened to the presence of

God. A revival service of sweat and work. A magnificent transformation. Such a glorious feeling yet so familiar; this reflection of my youth as I listened to the prattle of the preacher is now replaced with the patter of my feet. Could this be one and the same? Christ Jesus I feel good!

I float along, filled with ecstasy. I wave to the disciples offering water but I do not partake. I feel divine and immortal. Thank you, I say, thank you, oh Lord, for I run toward the bright light. But just as the familiar hymns faded from the revival, ever so slowly, I begin to sense the reality of my place. The patter becomes hammering and the goal becomes distant. As if God is drifting from my soul I begin to feel alone and forsaken. Pain replaces peace and the devil begins to smirk. All manner of hostilities play on my mind and body as I think of the biblical Job. Is God testing me with a diabolical contest? I will not give in, I will not fall back.

As I cross the line drawn in the sand by some sadistic hand, I look fleetingly for God's warmth and comfort to return. I am startled by the silver blanket being wrapped around me by an unknown marine as he leads me to sustenance and rest. I stare at the young man, a soldier trained to pour havoc upon his enemy, to kill without hesitation and I find kindness and cheer. Placed in a tent warmed by heated bodies, I ponder these things in my heart. Is it all a phenomenon that has no meaning? A rainbow explained by water drops and sunlight. Rock of Ages or ages of rocks? There is no answer. I have run to Agnostos and I will run again. And if it's all the same, I prefer my feet to the preacher any day.

JOHN A. CANTRILL is an insurance broker from Philadelphia. His religion is thinking and his addiction is running.

Eastern Tracks

Ana Yoerg

The soft strains of unidentified music come in through the half-open window, barely audible over the whirring of the fan that stirs the damp night air. A cock begins to crow, but stops short in a choked gargle of surprise.

I crack open my eyes; they fall upon a jagged line of minuscule ants steadily making their way up the wall, parting only to circumvent the cracks in the yellowed plaster. A daring gecko scampers across the wall and disappears behind the faded curtain. Soft, plum-colored sunshine bathes the twisted sheets in light, and I slowly prop myself up on my elbows and peer out the window.

Outside, and all over the world, millions of people remain wrapped in the watery womb of sleep. They grasp the corners of the sheets and twist them around their sleeping bodies, playfully resisting the inevitable wakefulness of the day. Yet even when they do rise, they are often not really awake. It is a phenomenon known as the waking life of mortal men: to wallow in the memories of the past, project thoughts far into the future, but not know how to really and truly *be* in the present.

Centuries ago, however, one man roused himself, shook off the daze, and wiped the sleep from his eyes. This man is known as the

Buddha. The Pali root word *budh* means "to be enlightened" or "awake." It is not a name, it is a title. It is not something you are born with, like a King or a Duke, but rather something you earn through understanding and awareness.

Young Siddhartha Gotama earned this title through deep and meaningful meditation. He sat immobile under a tree in the dense forest of Bodhgaya province in India, oblivious to everything but his thoughts. Throughout the night, he meditated upon the human condition of suffering, and as the mellow light of dawn broke over the horizon, Siddhartha opened his eyes and saw things from a new perspective. He saw the truth about himself, the truth about the human condition, and the truth about reality. In a word, he awoke.

And here I am. I'm sitting ten floors above the city of Chiang Mai in northern Thailand. I'm awake, and I'm ready for my morning run.

Today it's cockfighting. Yesterday it was drag racing. Each time I cut through the vast parking lot behind my building, there is some unusual event going on. One time, I spied a group of elderly Thai men drinking whiskey and watching the U.S. Open underneath a hastily constructed tin roof . . . at seven in the morning.

I weave through the semicircular wooden cages that dot the pavement like lids on a pressure cooker, their contents squawking, ready to bubble over in a violent outburst of beaks and feathers. I try to ignore their sufferings but my heart sinks in compassion for them— and I am reminded of what the Buddha taught—we are all one, and the suffering of other beings is also our own.

I head toward the mountains that flank the west side of this city of 1.5 million, in which 85 percent of the people call themselves Buddhists. Temples are the center of Thai religious life, and it is through the daily exploration of my local temples that I have found my spiritual center and most valuable lessons.

The first on the route is Wat Phra That Doi Suthep. It is nestled in the mountains, which on this particular morning appear to be a child's diorama, complete with crumpled Astroturf hills, toothpick trees, and a low-hanging gray cotton mist. I fix my gaze upon it as a goal to run toward, much needed, as it is a slow uphill climb to the foothills. My lungs scream in protest as I churn through the early morning traffic, breathing in the acrid vehicular exhaust. They want oxygen, and I'm giving them carbon monoxide. Also, my body is not warmed up yet; I clench my stomach as the slight chill of the air raises goose bumps on my bare skin.

Of course, it's not cold, not really. It's probably about sixty-five degrees, but my acclimatized body doesn't know the difference between this and a brisk autumn morning. Neither do the groups of Thais huddled around piles of burning garbage, kindling, and giant teak leaves, wrapped in winter coats and hats. The whites of their eyes stand out from dark faces as they stare unabashedly. They seem to say: *You are not like us.* I duck under overhanging branches, trimmed no higher than five and a half feet, the landscapers never dreaming that the paths would be traveled by anyone taller. Countless pairs of eyes follow my course.

Thai people don't run. Or walk. My Thai friend Kanjana, a spunky old woman who eats nothing but brown rice and pineapples, once told me their common saying about running: "Never run when you can walk. Never walk when you can ride." Why is this? Perhaps it's the heat, the pollution, or the lack of sidewalks. Everyone clearly thinks I'm crazy. "*Farang baa,*" I overhear from a group of male students standing by the rusted goalposts of a dusty soccer field. "Crazy foreigner."

The only Thais *not* staring at me are the ones I love the most. After sidling through a narrow gate, I turn onto the long stretch that approaches Wat Fay Hin. From here, I can barely see the *nagas*, or dragons, that frighteningly lavish the staircase leading up into the temple.

Directly in front of me are a single-file line of monks. Their shaven heads are bowed, and they clutch the edges of their saffron-colored robes close for warmth. They hold golden chrome alms bowls close to their tummies, like pregnant mothers supporting their babies. From behind, I can see that the pads of their bare feet are well worn, the color of asphalt, from the daily 6 A.M. walk to the city to collect offerings from the community. My heart, throbbing from exertion, now fills with wonderment at the people's generosity, for the bowls teem with aromatic curries, steaming bags of cooked rice, and glass bottles of soy milk.

The monks' quiet demeanor instills a strange feeling of peace in me, despite my gasping breath and pounding feet. They seem to maintain an immovable center of gravity, a sacred inner pivot point that keeps their innermost self as still as night, even while everything on the outside is in motion. The effect is contagious; I feel as if inside I am as tranquil as they are, though the wide fronds of palm trees are blurry as I run by, and I know that I am moving.

As I pass on the right-hand side, I carefully avoid brushing into them, for a touch from a woman would send them into hours of guilt-filled prayers. My deference does not go by unnoticed. Several of them gently shy away from my passing form, avoiding lustful gazes at bare legs and a teasingly long blond ponytail.

The lane widens and empties out onto a dirt track that encircles the third temple on my route, Wat Umong. Built in the 1380s by King Ku Na for a brilliant but deranged monk named Jan, it is by far the most unique temple in Chiang Mai. Hand-painted Buddhist maxims are posted on the trees in the compound, tunnels underneath the main building crisscross each other and dead-end in walls of brick, and the man-made lake is filled with thrashing bodies of overfed carp. An anonymous voice gives nonstop dharma lectures over tinny loudspeakers.

The strangest part of this temple is a grotesque black statue of the Buddha during his six years of fasting and self-mortification. The protruding ribs and veins are a clear lesson to avoid such ascetic extremes. As the Buddha discovered, we should follow the Middle Path. Nothing too much or too little, too fast or too slow. (In other words, we need to find the porridge that Goldilocks ate.) This, he says, is the true path to enlightenment.

It is a path, though, that many serious runners would hesitate to follow. After all, aren't "extremes" what running is all about? Pushing yourself to your absolute limit? I begin to wonder if this is why Buddhists don't run. The Western ideal of "work hard, play hard" encourages activities like jogging because of the intense physical and emotional experiences it can offer. We talk about the "runner's high" and the "runner's low," getting your "second wind" and "sprinting the final stretch." Buddhists would laugh at all of this foolishness. And they would gently remind us of the long-forgotten credo: Slow and steady wins the race. In the Eastern mind, though, such a race does not even exist.

Coming into the "last stretch" of my own "race," however, it's obvious that I've not yet fully adopted the Buddhist mentality. There is a new fire in my legs as I zoom past pad thai vendors and toothless old women squatting on plastic stools, snapping green beans. Entering the expat district, the thatched huts give way to white mansions, hemmed in by iron gates and panting German shepherds.

But I pay no attention to any of this, staring straight ahead at the unchanging pavement. The outside environment blends into nothingness, and all of my concentration is bent inward. I feel like I can run forever.

Sitting cross-legged inside the meditation temple that I now pass is a man, eyes closed, completely still. A fly lands on his knee but goes unnoticed. Look closely at him. He is concentrating solely on the rising and falling of his breath. As he breathes in, he is thinking to himself, *rising,* and as he breathes out, he is thinking, *falling.* His concentration is bent inward, and he feels like he could sit there forever.

Suddenly, the sound of crunching banana leaves comes to his ears, coupled with the heavy breathing of a runner. His senses are so heightened that he can pinpoint exactly how fast this runner is approaching and he anticipates the current of air that will follow her passing, lifting the perspiration from his brow and cooling his forehead. He acknowledges the sensation, then returns to his breath. "Rising. Falling."

Many people say that a runner's high is the separation of your mind from your body, therefore feeling no pain, and subsequently being empowered to "run forever." But what I've learned through *vipassana,* or insight meditation, is that a true runner's high is not *losing* touch with your physical body, but *gaining awareness* of it. You are more aware of your physical limitations than ever before. And your mind is one-pointed, yes, but rather than focusing on far-off thoughts like last night's dream or today's errands, you are contemplating your deep breaths, your burning leg muscles, the trickles of sweat behind your ears. Deep awareness of all this is true understanding of suffering. And as the Buddha said, "Suffering and joy are one and the same." That is a true runner's high.

I've heard people describe running as their "escape" from the real world. I've also heard people describe Eastern religion, philosophy, and meditation as an escape from the real world. In my opinion, neither of these is true.

A Vietnamese Buddhist monk named Thich Nhat Han once wrote, "We do not practice meditation to escape. We practice to have enough strength to confront problems effectively." When are Buddhists the most clearheaded, the most capable of dealing with the real world? After a meditation session. When are runners the strongest? After a good, long jog.

I love Thailand, and I love the strength that my Buddhist-centered running gives me. Kanjana thinks I'll never go back home. "You are not same-same foreigner," she says in her broken English. "You will stay to learn more about Buddhism and meditation, to make you strong."

But I will. I miss running in cold winter air, fellow joggers to salute and give encouragement, and sidewalks that don't have random gaps and downed electrical wires to dodge. I miss blending into the crowd, not having every move be monitored by stares of wonderment. More than this, I miss my family and my friends.

Oh yes, I'll go home. But I'm bringing Buddha with me.

ANA YOERG is a freelance writer, teacher, and traveler. She has written for *Chiang Mai Citylife, The Irrawaddy,* and completed a gift book of job advice for recent college graduates. She is currently holding down three jobs of her own in order to afford living in Manhattan, where you might find her hunting for authentic Thai food or devilishly carousing on the running paths of Central Park.

Running from Sadness

Adrian S. Potter

As a boy, I always believed that if I could run fast enough, my sadness would never be able to catch up to me. It is unclear whether that was a clever theory, or if I was simply a delusional child. Either way, running provided me with the quiet confidence to convert obstacles into opportunities. It gave me a framework to cope with the awkwardness of youth and a way to deal with the inevitable surprises of growing up in a competitive world. Whether I was playing sports or avoiding the menacing threats of playground bullies, I sprinted as if I was escaping the grasp of personal anguish. For me, there was no better reason for trying to become a champion.

But as time unraveled, this string of running from sadness was methodically abandoned, stored somewhere in the hall closet alongside the other souvenirs from childhood. Adults are often compelled to toss aside the things that we enjoy most in order to become dull and responsible. That may sound like a brutal process, but society merely calls it maturation. It became increasingly easy to overlook running as I became infatuated with career goals, monthly bills, weekly laundry, and the educated laughter of aristocrats. My legs slowly stopped moving with fast-paced strides, and the rhythmic lullaby of my shoes pounding on city pavement became a rare, unfamiliar noise. I forgot how easy it was to flee from the subtle gloom that now consumed my days.

It is mid-September, the month of scales and equilibrium, yet my world feels dangerously unbalanced. I am only twenty-eight years old, but I have already found myself imagining defeat and flinching at the responsibilities of daily existence. I have been held hostage by my own ambition, and my failures have started to feel final. The pain of a father who passed away and the burden of a broken relationship that failed like a child's science experiment both push down on my spirit. The neon sign outside my window blinks the indifference of urban seasons. Despite the suffocating, stormy twilight and my misplaced thoughts, instinct is luring me outdoors, beckoning me to embrace physical activity as a form of private therapy.

Drawn by this unfathomable need to venture into the city nightscape, I tentatively step outside my apartment. The crisp air and cool precipitation greet me unceremoniously. Nothing about this environment seems friendly or motivating. Undaunted, I begin my journey, starting with a few quick steps and no true destination. Since running had provided me with the secondhand inspiration I craved during my childhood, I hope that tonight, while I dash through this downpour, I can again outdistance my sadness.

I deliberately groan down the street in pain, lurching across town like a wounded soldier or a rusted sedan. With only sharp winds and humid air to keep me company, my lungs struggle to maintain a sufficient pace of breathing. My muscles tighten and act unresponsive as they resist the athletic movements that were once natural. Part of me wants to concede and seek refuge underneath that comfortable fleece blanket on my couch. But I push on, clumsily splashing through puddles and potholes. As I continue to move, my sweatshirt soon becomes stained with sweat and the scent of my efforts. My thighs and calves seemingly relax, rediscovering how to function without cramping. My shoes carefully study the concrete sidewalks, creating a soulful beat with raw percussion. What was once forgotten was now relearned, and therefore appreciated.

The silence of the nighttime can provide vocal answers to the most difficult questions of life. To me, running is victory redefined: the concept of being able to leave my sadness far behind me, hunkered over and wheezing on some desolate street corner. It is what transforms basic exercise into a sacred addiction. The rain, my gossiping friend, watches this private triumph and announces it to the world by bouncing additional droplets onto windowpanes. Ignoring my fragile stamina, I continue navigating through alleys and avenues, wildly darting through neighborhoods as if I were a hyperactive kid just released from after-school detention.

With my troubles behind me, I streak toward the sanctity of home, seeking shelter and warmth. Although I envision running forever, the reality of my recent inactivity has conspired to abruptly interrupt that dream. I am now exhausted. As I unlock the door to my modest apartment, I smile knowing that sadness will never be welcome at this address again, even if it could somehow catch up to me.

ADRIAN S. POTTER lives in Minneapolis, where he works as a consultant and plays by writing poetry and short stories. He has been published in several literary journals and won first place in the 2003 Langston Hughes Poetry Contest.

Marathon Day: Angels, Chariots, and Isaiah 40:31

Gerry Bell

When I retired to a coastal Maine island from a high-pressure consulting job ten years ago, I gave up running. I didn't become sedentary; I just substituted skiing, windsurfing and swimming for my four-times-a-week run. Even though I had run in some breathtaking countryside—the Somerset Hills in New Jersey and the Hudson River Palisades—the running itself wasn't beautiful for me. I did it for fitness, weight control, and stress reduction; just another grim check-off on my Type A "to do" list. The runner's high was a myth, I thought: a polite term for some smug sense of superiority felt by the really lean, fit, fast runners. For me, running was effort, not joy, so I quit.

But skiing is seasonal, swimming laps in a pool is boring, and the windsurfing waters of Casco Bay are brutally cold, even in summer. Last April, the thought occurred to me that I could stay in shape between ski seasons by running. Good exercise. Stay fit. Maybe even sweat off a few pounds.

Alas, the Type A personality never dies. We need goals, so how about the Maine Marathon in October? If I start at the end of ski season in April, then six months is just enough for a training period; and since the marathon is the ultimate, I won't have to worry about my time. Our island is small—only three miles around the perimeter road—but indescribably beautiful. Maybe for once I can enjoy running.

Naturally, I start by letting my impatience get the better of me. I increase my weekly mileage way too fast, get hurt—everything seems to hurt; ankle, knee, hip, Achilles, everything—and I can't run without pain until late July. The marathon is gone. Maybe the half-marathon, run at the same time, is possible. But, while I'm pain-free, the running is drudgery. I'm really slow. I'm abysmally slow. Time *does* matter in a half-marathon, and I won't run it if I'm going to humiliate myself.

My neighbor Patti, a runner herself, says I'm being silly. Honestly, she says. You *men*. Stop being so macho. The goal is just to finish; the joy is in the accomplishment. Besides, she says, be proud of yourself—no one else out here is running it, are they? Well, maybe Patti ought to be a motivational speaker, but I'm still not going to run this thing if I'm going to finish back with the great-grandmothers and the five-year-olds.

I get my training mileage—slowly this time—up to fifty miles a week, with a ten-mile time trial every Sunday. Things start to come together. I begin to think I can beat the humiliation threshold. The Type A demon who lives inside me suggests something better than that—maybe five minutes better, something that might be "respectable."

And then something odd happens. In my last time trial a week before the race, I start . . . floating. I feel almost unconscious. Everything just . . . *flows* . . . without effort, without thought. For the first time in my life, I don't look at my watch at every checkpoint.

Except when I finish. The demon reasserts himself, and I check my time. How strange. It turns out this "effortless" time trial produces a fabulous time! The demon and I now harbor thoughts of something even better, something five minutes faster than "respectable." This is the Time I Secretly Hope For. It is my deepest secret. I tell it to no one, not even my wife, Jackie.

Then, disaster. Following an easy jog a few days before the race, I'm struck with excruciating pain in my foot. I'll learn later that it's a classic case of plantar fasciitis, but right now all I know is that my foot hurts so much I can barely walk. I have to stay off it to have any hope of racing. But if I don't train, I'll lose my edge. Back to thoughts of humiliation.

Race day. Cool dawn and a cloudless sky. Perfect weather for a PR for everyone but me. My friend Ted gives me a ride in to the Portland waterfront on his boat. My foot still hurts; I feel like a man going to his own execution. Still, I have to try. I haven't come this far not to try.

Warming up, I jog a hundred yards. Maybe I can bear the pain if my Type A friend kicks in, my adrenaline pumps, and the crowd cheers. The loudspeakers blare the theme from *Rocky*. That's good, I think, but the theme from *Chariots of Fire* would be more inspiring.

I always start toward the back of the pack; to me it's always been a big lift to pass lots of people in the early going. But Baxter Boulevard in Portland is narrow, and it's packed with runners. I run beside the road, on the footpath around Back Cove. My footsteps whisper on the cinders. I feel good. I'm running alongside a woman who's running effortlessly. She's doing the marathon—"my first and only one," she says. I tell her she'll do fine; she's really running easily. She says she's just trying to keep herself from going out too fast. Then she pulls away. I feel inadequate, and now I'm aware of my foot again.

We cross Washington Avenue to head out Route 1. The police and volunteers and firemen are all shouting encouragement. "Looking good!" they all say. I figure this to be a lie. The guys at the front of the pack are looking good. I'm back with the plodders. But then I look at the people around me and they *are* looking good. Maybe I do, too . . .

We pass through four miles and I look at my watch. Wow. Something mysterious happened while I wasn't paying attention. I'm doing better than humiliation pace, better than respectable, better even than Secretly Hoped For. I'm flirting with the impossible here!

Alone on Route 1, I come upon a woman by the side of the road whose boom box is playing "Chariots of Fire." She's all by herself, and there's no particular reason for her to be where she is. She must be an angel. Her chariots carry me a few hundred yards, and I catch my marathoning friend. Has she gone out too fast, and is now tiring? No; she's still floating. In fact, so am I. The strange feeling that suffused me on my last time trial returns. I don't think about my time, or my pace, or my foot. Together my friend and I cross the town line from Falmouth to . . . Nirvana.

And then back again. As the lead half-marathoners reach their turnaround and head back, a woman running behind us craves the celebrity that she supposes will come with her knowing all the locals among the pacesetters. She calls out to them, loudly. "Hi Julie!! Looking great, Larry!! Way to go, Sarah!!" She's unbelievably disruptive. Our effortless floating crashes to earth. I toy with the idea of homicide as a public service. My friend mutters, "Can't that idiot shut up?" Never mind, I say. Everyone will shut up within a couple of miles—it's getting hot.

We reach the half-marathon turnaround. Good luck, I murmur to my friend. Thanks, she says; you too. She's still running easily. I'm envious. I wish I could float like that. She disappears down the marathon route. I wonder—does she have some kind of secret?

Over to Ocean Avenue and the hills. At the ten-mile mark is the long hill the locals call The Crusher. My pace slows a bit; the impossible time has slipped away. But as I the reach the top, a strange peace settles over me. I'm going a little slower, but I'm not discouraged, not exhausted. The act of running is now more important than the realization, which barely registers, that my pace is still ninety seconds ahead of the Time Secretly Hoped For.

Back across Washington Avenue and the volunteers. I notice we're not "looking good!" anymore; now it's "doing great!" and "way to go!" But it's still encouragement, and it's appreciated—because, with two miles to go, the temperature's rising quickly, and my foot hurts like fury.

Until this day my last mile in a race has been my fastest. The adrenaline surges, the crowd cheers, and besides, I've always run strategically dumb races. Lots of energy at the end means not enough given to the road during the race. But not this time. I've left it all out there. I'm whipped. It's a shame; I've tried so hard, and so has the demon. He's stoked my competitive fires, made me grit my teeth, fight through the pain in my foot, battle the heat—and it's all going to be for naught. I'm going to fail. I might not even finish.

Except then, unexpectedly, I hear a voice, as if a new running companion were at my shoulder. Is this an illusion, an auditory hallucination? Is it a trick of memory, summoned from a long forgotten verse on an old running poster? Or is it some magical, supernatural waking dream?

The voice belongs to Isaiah, first prophet of the Old Testament. Relax, he whispers. Have a little faith in yourself. Remember my prophecy. *"They that wait upon the Lord shall renew their strength; they shall mount up with wings as eagles; they shall run, and not be weary."*

Something inside me becomes immeasurably lighter. I not only maintain my pace, I increase it a little. This isn't simply adrenaline pumping; it's more than that. Maybe it's the joy in the accomplishment that Patti told me about—or something else entirely. My chin comes up, my shoulders square, my knees lift, my feet glide across the ground as they did at the race's start. I float across the finish line— Surprise, surprise! Twenty-five seconds under my Secret Time!—and just for a minute, nothing hurts at all . . .

I pass through the finishing chute with my running contemporaries. No one's paying us much attention; we are, after all, also-rans. But there's a woman in a Red Cross jacket at the end of the chute; she's obviously there to check for dehydration and heat exhaustion. She takes my hand—she takes *everyone's* hand—looks me in the eye, and says "Congratulations. Great race." And she means it. My heart soars. She must be sister to the Chariots of Fire angel out on the Falmouth Road, and to the angel who floated alongside me the first half of the race.

My euphoria vanishes when Monday's newspaper lists the order of finish. I'm in the top half, but not by much. The demon takes note of this. And here are a couple of names that have No Business being ahead of mine. The demon rages. This Is Not Acceptable. This Will Never Happen Again. I should go out running right now . . .

And so I do. But a mile out, on a deserted island road ablaze with fall foliage at its peak, my emotions subside. I'm enjoying this. The soreness from the race is gone. I have skiing to look forward to now, along with running. And maybe next year, just maybe, there might be a marathon. Sure, I'll have a time in mind, a time I won't even tell Jackie. I can't help that; I am who I am, and the demon can't be completely exorcised. But now I know that the time will be secondary to the journey, to the experience.

And maybe, if I'm patient, if I let it happen instead of trying to force it, maybe that mystical, otherworldly, out-of-body feeling will come over me on some of my long training runs, or even on race day itself. Maybe I will again be visited by the prophet Isaiah, and he will once more bring angels, and chariots, and joy.

GERRY BELL spent last winter skiing the Rockies and adapting a play for the Great Diamond Island summer theater troupe. He is now back on the island roads, training for the Maine Marathon, rehearsing his lines for the play, and trying to savor the whole experience. Meanwhile, his demon is intent on qualifying for Boston . . .

I Could Run Forever

David G. Grant

Runner's high; I feel as if I could run forever; every part of my being working in unison with nature, nothing feeling pieced together like so many of the puzzles of day-to-day life. I feel almost naked, not at all exposed or unsafe, but free.

I feel no shoes, nothing too tight; no laces binding, no heel sliding, no toes rubbing, no stones jabbing, socks just there to keep my feet comfortably in place. The soles of my shoes just touching the pavement, gliding, no sliding, no slipping, it feels nearly like I run without contact, more like running on a road paved with clouds but without resistance, and no bounding or bouncing. My feet move one in front of the other and strike the ground with perfect form, not plodding along, but moving in motion like an elliptical on a moving walkway. My shorts sway in a flowing motion; a cool breeze ripples them from side to side as my legs swing forward and back. My shirt sways over my shoulders, the sleeves like bells around my arms, the body rides loosely around my chest and waist. No sweat trickles down my face; no salt dries to my lips, my shirt doesn't feel pasted to me.

The wind is just right, cool, but not cold, stiff but not battling against me, a slight tailwind, enough to lighten my feet but not even enough to make the hair on my ankles stand upright. The sun shines brightly; my eyes look upward to a perfect sky with wisps of high white clouds painting over a sky so blue I know where they got the name of Carolina blue; I am reminded why this is a great place to live.

No cars zip by, no horns to make my heart skip a beat, no noisy interruptions of music passing by, no trucks to make the pavement rumble and the air smell oily.

I can smell the warmth of summer, the crisp air of autumn, the moistness of spring, the dry icy emptiness of winter. I breathe effortlessly, in through my nose, out through my mouth, in my mouth, out my nose, the air tastes clean and each breath seems to nourish. There is no labor in my breath; none of that is a part of my consciousness, not now; I never feel winded, I run with a smile. My eyes are wide open looking around, not watching my surroundings trying to be prepared for whatever I might encounter, but rather just scanning the horizon, observing the beauty and the intricacies of the world, the rugged streets flow to soft corners of curbs, the curbs to smooth sidewalks, the sidewalks to lush green yards, yards to tall stately trees; I hear a dog bark, a bird chirp, children playing.

It's early in the morning, with crisp quiet air and spring dewdrops; the sun begins to wake and warm the lazy morning. The afternoon heat wraps me, and the world exudes and hints of lazy summer days. It's a premature autumn dusk; the air is starting to smell of night, the clouds glow orange in front of the harvest moon. It's bright as the sun reflects off the new-fallen snow; my breath leaves a trail like fading bread crumbs in the air. Daffodils sway in the breeze, blades of freshly cut grass trickle in the gutter, leaves dance in rich colors across my path, bare tree branches rattle like wind chimes. It's spring, the air is heavy and wet, it just stopped raining; it's just about to restart. The soles of my shoes scatter raindrops across wet asphalt. My arms sway at my side. I wave to the neighbors. I smile. They smile back.

There is no race; there is no clock, no odometer, no pedometer, no speedometer, no start line, no finish line, no one to race against, no one to pass, no one to be passed by. No timers beeping, no pace alarms, no television, no phones ringing, no music blaring, just the rhythm of my feet, heart, and breath all moving in harmony, all working together. I could run forever. I think I will run forever, no hurry, no headache, no heartache. I won't be thirsty, water will be provided, energy gel aplenty. No RSVP, no T-shirt lines, no packet pickup, no one to step in front of you in the corral. I have no ambition, I'm full of ambition. I feel like I could run forever. The runner's high.

DAVID GRANT lives, runs, cycles, works, and writes in Charlotte, North Carolina, with his wife, Brianna, and their two dogs, Albus, the Lab mix who likes to run short distances fast, and Fiona, the boxer who likes to run slow, or maybe just walk.

Memorial Run

Carisa L. Heiney

It was a clear but blustery January day. However, I would have been happier to see dark menacing clouds or maybe a thick choking fog to match my mood. Two weeks had passed since I had done anything besides walk slowly with my dog. I convinced myself I would be happy even if I only ran for ten minutes. Yet I secretly pleaded with the sky that if I looked outside again and suddenly saw a foot of unplowed snow on the ground I would run every day for a week starting tomorrow. No deal, so with my hat, mittens, and very little willpower I walked out the door. Once outside, the only urge I had was to run back inside. No, I needed to run; I wanted to run I told myself. I am still a runner. Running by myself always gave me the opportunity to think and reflect on my life. I typically relished this time and found solutions to many of my questions. Now, though, I dreaded the thought of running alone. I dreaded being alone with my thoughts because all I could think about was my loss. I was in constant need of distractions.

However, I started to run slowly, very slowly; I might as well have been walking for as slow as I was plodding along. I couldn't go any faster; I could barely go at all. My resources were diminished, and soon I was walking with small tears streaming down my face. I had no idea I had anything left in me to generate tears, but there they were again. The physical and emotional pain were completely intertwined in me. I was too emotionally drained to have any physical energy left. I questioned what made me imagine I was ready and able to run. For the billionth time in the past two weeks, I was overwhelmed with my sadness and anger over my grandfather's death. I felt guilty wanting to do anything for my selfish pleasure. How could I possibly think of doing something so trivial like running?

I tried running again; it was painful, but I managed to run to the end of the block before I felt like stopping again. Funny, I thought to myself, two weeks ago I had done mile repeats on the treadmill. Now I just wanted to be able to finish one mile without breaking down. I felt like an elephant was sitting on my chest, and that someone had filled my shoes with concrete. I suddenly stopped at the tree stump Pap Pap used to rest on, joking that it was a perfect seat for his tired legs. The wind dried most of my tears as they fell, leaving stinging trails on my face. I choked on my emotions, willing myself to make it just a bit farther.

Before I knew it, though, I arrived at a place that reminded me of you, a place almost too sacred to visit without you. I instinctively sprinted up what I called "baby hill." I felt my forgotten leg muscles spring to life. It was too easy, so I jogged to "granddaddy hill" and my shaky legs carried me to the peak without any shred of mental energy. As I jogged back down, I questioned how I made it to the top, why I even attempted it. I certainly could not do it again, for I was too shattered and exhausted. Again I found myself at the top of the hill. Rationally I knew I would be sore the next day. I knew I would not approve of any of the athletes I coached doing a hill workout after a two-week hiatus. In fact, I would say it was a pretty senseless decision, but at that time I did not care. I did not care about physical pain, for it could be nothing compared to the pain I felt when you suddenly passed away three days before Christmas. Besides, it was not like I was actually making a conscious decision to do hill repeats; my legs were doing it all on their own. I had no choice but to follow them.

I crested the top again and again. Finally, after so many hills that I lost count, I stopped at the top where I could see over the trees. A lone eagle soared above me as if to congratulate me on my accomplishment. In that instant I began to smile at the thought of Pap Pap and me watching my puppy play on top of that very hill. As all the happy times I had with my grandfather came back to me, I heard a sound that almost seemed foreign to me, my own laughter. Soon my face actually hurt from smiling; even though I'm sure the cold, windy day played a part in that. My spirits were soaring just like that eagle above me.

For the past two weeks I had survived on autopilot. I had felt empty, alone, and listless; I could not remember what I felt before Pap Pap died. After feeling a lingering coldness that penetrated every muscle and bone in my body, I now felt cleansed of that iciness. A gentle flame had ignited and was slowly surging through me. As I slowly jogged home I reflected on my impromptu hill workout and realized that after years of purposefully going through the motions of running, my muscles had been able to revive not only my ability to run, but also my spirit. It was by sheer memory that my muscles carried me up and down that hill because I certainly did not make a thoughtful decision to do it. I barely believed I had the energy to run around the block. Never would I have imagined that I was that resilient.

My body, my machine, had decided that what I needed most that day was to feel alive. How could I not feel alive when every muscle in my body was working to get me up those hills? The lasting pain in my muscles reminded me that yes, I was still alive inside. I had almost forgotten what it felt like to feel any positive emotions. Never again would I consider running insignificant or replaceable in my life. It was something that brought me great happiness. It was something that made me feel alive. In the past maybe some days I took it for granted, but I was now more cognizant of the purpose running had in my life. I was indeed still strong, and it was time for me to live again.

When CARISA L. HEINEY is not writing she often runs with her husband, Brian, or walks with her dog, Olive. This professional pet-sitter owns her own business and dedicates every spring to coaching high school track and field.

The Gift

Chanty Ruth Netting

It was dark outside my home in Akron, Ohio. But this was no deterrent to my idea of a run that evening. I lived along Interstate 77 with my husband where there was plenty of light for my evening run. Winter had come and there was snow on the ground. It would be so pleasant running over the soft surface of the snow. The snow fell gently in large, diverse flakes. It was simply too beautiful to stay inside. So out I went into the snow for a beautiful evening run.

The night was cold and it promised to get colder still. I could hardly wait. I loved to run in the cool of the night, feeling colder at the end than I had at the beginning. These were ideal conditions for me. The gentle snow falling on my head while I plunged along over the soft terrain was so delightful. How could anyone stay inside on a night like this? But in they did stay as I ran along doing laps around my neighborhood with only me to enjoy the wonder of it all. But I wasn't completely alone, as I would soon discover this miraculous night.

The temperature plummeted as I passed my home again and again. I was smiling as I ran lap after lap of the 1.3-mile course I had measured out. I would run two laps and then switch directions. It was so good to be out in the chill night air.

On and on I ran as minutes turned into a half hour and an hour turned into an hour and a half. I didn't want this run to ever end even though I was experiencing the cold chill in my bones. How beautiful were the snowflakes in the streetlights of the interstate. The cars flew by and the occupants had no idea of the joy I was experiencing. I marveled at how the surface became cleaner and softer with each step I ran as the snow continued its downward spiral.

All at once I felt a sudden glow from deep within my soul. All was well with the world. It didn't feel quite so cold. My speed may even have picked up. Whatever worries may have plagued me vanished suddenly and completely. Was this the runner's high I had read about and heard about from others? I felt at peace with my surroundings. I felt a deep love for what God had provided me. He had given me the gift of running after all. I felt a complete sense of satisfaction that this was something God meant me to experience with Him. He had brought me out on this cold night to run with Him and find more happiness than I thought I could know.

On and on we ran, my God and I. Lap after lap the joy grew in leaps and bounds. I didn't stop. I couldn't stop. I was finding that deep sense of satisfaction knowing that all would be fine as long as I had Him by my side matching my steps and my stride. Sometimes He would lunge ahead of me, and with a wave, beckon me to follow His lead and surge ahead. This was contentment through and through. This was the music of feet dancing on the pavement outside my home as surely the angels danced in Heaven. This was a blessing beyond compare. Yes, life was good, and I was so happy to have my Lord to thank for His divine goodness.

At long last, I slowed to a walk. My cold face was creased into a pleasant smile. I felt as though I were floating now with my feet high above the snow-filled clouds. My soul was enraptured with the pure joy of being alive and knowing Him. This was how He had meant me to feel all the time. I couldn't wait to go inside and phone my husband at work and tell him of the joy I had found that evening.

I still run, though not necessarily at night anymore. My dear husband has been gone six years now—a victim of melanoma that invaded his brain. I smile as I write these words remembering how God taught me to feel His joy and His love. I am warmed through the pain and separation of loss just remembering that night so long ago running with my Lord.

My running still serves the purpose of relief from my sorrow. It helps me through my own battle with fibromyalgia. I awake and find myself in pain. I dress and lace up my shoes and set off for my run with God. Though I may feel pain at first, it soon vanishes as I feel the comfort of the runner's high I experienced long ago on a snowy night in Akron, Ohio. The pain of loss vanishes as I am carried away with the wonder of being able to run at all. And I always ask God to tell my husband how He and I had a wonderful and joyous run together that day.

CHANTY RUTH NETTING lives in Newark, Ohio.

Open Your Heart

Kitty A. Consolo

Her tenth anniversary was July 21, 2001. I'm speaking of the ten-year anniversary since my mom died after a fourteen-year-long battle with cancer. She told me that she didn't want a funeral and that her death must be a celebration of her life. Yet the harsh reality that she wasn't coming back left a sorrow so deep in my heart that there was little room for joy. People tell you that after six months or a year's time, much of grief heals. It hadn't happened that way with me. I had turned to the things that had always lifted me before, my music and my running. But even those activities that once ignited my spirit left me feeling exhausted and heavy. The more time that elapsed after her death, the farther away joy and healing were for me. It seemed that the best of my life was behind me. I was going through the motions, and even running had become a monotonous motion with no feeling. My heart had turned to stone and I was tired of carrying it around. I never felt more alone . . .

I decided it was time for a run in the bio reserve. The bio reserve is sacred as it is devoid of cars and usually people. It is several acres of safety and familiarity; my place of refuge and comfort when the outside world becomes too much. I don't know why, but I had not run there in years.

My feet carried me to the lower fields first. I crossed the wooden footbridge and gazed at the small creek. Just then the sun caught the wings of a dragonfly, and it looked like it was made of gold threads. It rested on the water with ease and I envied its journey: Why couldn't my life flow with joy like that? I asked. I ran toward the field and saw several spiderwebs covered with the morning dew. The sun rays caught these drops so vividly that I had to stop and admire them; they appeared as real diamonds, shimmering with miniature rainbows inside. In that instant, I felt a flutter in my heart, the flutter of excitement and awe in the discovery of those riches of His Kingdom. I flashed back to being three years old and seeing a butterfly land on a morning glory. I had raced back to tell my parents . . . *but I can't tell her now,* I thought." I was good at reminding myself of my loss! I came to a dead stop and thought, *Why go on . . .*

I looked up across the field, and there were large streams of sun rays pouring down on the fields. Butterflies were visiting the many flowers in bloom when I heard the voice say, "She can still hear you . . . she is with you on another plane . . ." I began to run slowly toward the sun rays until the path itself was under full sun. I felt such a warmth on my skin—but this time my heart felt it too. "You will feel the joy you seek when you open your heart," the voice said. I put my hand on my heart and continued to run down the sunlit path. Like the proverbial lightbulb that goes on in your head when you "get it," the light began to glow in my heart; I really had not realized how I had allowed my grief and loss to close my heart. It seemed that no matter how hard I would run, my heart had felt dead and heavy. Now I felt my heart had sprouted wings. Though I was coming to a steep hill, my legs effortlessly carried me up the path.

A doe and two fawns ran out in front of me. Now, the grief part of me would have said, *Even they have a mother!*, but instead I stared at them with awe and continued up the hill then down and out toward the center of the reserve. Just as I hit the grassy areas I felt enveloped in a warm breeze, and I heartily ran into it. I quickened my pace just for the joy and found my stride to be effortless and connected with the earth. It was just after that when the unexpected happened. The heavy stone of grief that I had been carrying in my heart dissolved. I cannot explain it, but inside my chest felt light. I laughed out loud and looked up to see a tiny rainbow sticking out from the clouds. I've heard that rainbows are God's promises of what lies in His Kingdom, and I felt that rainbow was my reminder that as a runner, I am blessed to share in His Kingdom in a specially connected way.

I do not know how it happened but I know it had to do with me allowing it to happen . . . of trusting that in the universe, I belong. I am connected. I am not alone and I really never had been until I allowed grief to close down my heart.

As I continued running through the center of the reserve, I felt a joy and high even winning major marathons had not brought me. This high was different because it wasn't just my physiology and emotions that felt it; my heart, spirit, and soul did, too. That day, I got a taste of Heaven on earth. That day, I felt my mom and her love and God's love—it was a warmth and light we receive when we open to His Kingdom.

Today I no longer search for those physiological highs. I run with my heart open, and I have had many running "spiritual highs" in the bio reserve. I faced tragedies like 9/11 and other losses with an open heart. I will not let pain and grief shut it down again. I live the path of love. I feel my mom's spirit and I talk to her often. I now have many loving friends, a loving husband, devoted dogs, and a renewed sense of faith and life. And when tragedies strike, I head for the bio reserve, where I run on the path of love and light.

DR. KITTY A. CONSOLO is a popular motivational speaker, writer, national-class runner and educator. She currently teaches many health classes, anatomy and physiology, and activity classes at Ohio University Zanesville Campus. Since 1975, she has won over four hundred races in distance running and continues to compete and win as a Masters runner.

Perhaps This Is Enough

Judy Wolf

"Why are you running?" I was asked this the other day by a practical-minded accomplisher of goals. "Are you planning to enter a marathon or something?"

Groping through the flimsy spiderwebs of logic that crowd this particular corner of my mind, I fumbled for an answer. "Gosh, I don't know, maybe someday I'll run a marathon."

I turned away from this exchange, vaguely disappointed. Discouraged. Uncertain where I fit into the world of achievement and accolades. Wondering what I could say for myself that would matter.

Loping the next morning through my favorite wooded glen, I ponder this question: "Why are you running?" After all, it is not something I am particularly good at.

On leafy autumn trails laced with early-morning frost, I squint into a low-lying sun that weeks ago fled south for winter. Bare, arched limbs of maple, ash, basswood, and black cherry etch their outlines into my peripheral vision. I inhale air rich with the musk of their dying leaves, flattened into a variegated carpet of burnt sienna along my muddy path.

I am not someone who has ever believed in God—except, perhaps, when I was nine, and desperate for meaning—I simply wasn't raised that way. I was, however, raised to think that hard work inevitably yields high achievement (and any shortfall therefore points unavoidably to individual failing). I have spent years laboring under the notion that school grades and athletic awards mean some people are better than others, that self-worth should be based on how one fares against the competition, and that I, me, myself, always deserve better.

In an hour, I will be stretched, showered, clothed, and seated at a computer monitor, networked to the world. I will do what I am good at: managing headstrong projects, roping them in like rampant steer, filling blank pages with words. I will prove myself, again and again, with each triumph over unruly ventures, and I will call myself fulfilled. But here, now, in these woods, what does it matter? Who am I among these trees?

"Why are you running?" I ponder it with my entire being—not just with my mind, in its solitary corner, grasping for words and conclusions—but with every ounce of my flesh: with my heart, beating in resonant response to each hill; with my skin, kissed by the crisp air of daybreak; with my arms, pumping, pumping; with my feet, agile over tumbled rocks, steady in their relentless rhythm; with my will, holding it all together. The question courses through my bloodstream, and—with my entire being—I answer it.

If I were to believe in God, it would be right here, in these enigmatic and interwoven woods, swept up in this heroic march through the seasons. How do I tell those rigorous, pragmatic people that I run for this moment between trees when rays strike out and I am blinded by the winter sun? That I run for this instant, eternally repeated, wherein I have no choice but to trust my own footfalls? I could stumble over any one of a multitude of roots, hidden beneath the treachery of leaves, but my imagination carries me forward, carving a place for me in time and space, persuaded I am important.

And then, as on most mornings, there comes the flicker, the shift into anonymity. The lines demarking one thing from another disintegrate. Every breath is interconnected. The rays of the sun, the blink of my eyes—they are one. The fall of my feet on the rutted, uneven earth echoes the beat of my heart. My scent mingles with the stench of recent bonfires and the sharp tang of sap retreating deep into tree trunks. I, we are preparing for winter, for the bottomless uncertainty of whether we will arise again come spring.

I turn on impulse down a trail I have never before taken, alert to possibility. There is no certainty, only this question of courage, suspended in the morning sky, implicit in the crackling of twigs underfoot: Can I bear not having an answer? I inhale cold, bright lungfuls of air; I listen between footfalls to the chittering of chickadees, bunched together to endure the coming snows; I gather myself to leap over a puddle rimed with ice. The ground slopes steeply downward, a ravine I will need to climb out of in the end. *Where is it taking me, this path?* And a moment later, *Does it matter?*

My footprints cease to hold any greater—or lesser—significance than the others that make pockmarks in my path, but they are here, and this simple fact is elemental: I exist.

JUDY WOLF (www.judywolf.com) is a freelance writer and world traveler currently working on her first book. Her writing has appeared in publications such as *Alpinist*, *Conservationist*, and *Hope Magazine*, in addition to the anthologies *Far From Home* and *A Woman's Europe*.

Running for My Life

Nick Ullett

I know why I watch marathons on TV, but I can't imagine why other people do. It's a strange sort of sports coverage when you think of it. There's nothing much to see and little or no suspense. Groups of runners pound through urban settings that seem remarkably alike no matter where they're running. It makes me wonder: How many people actually have a stake in who wins a marathon? A handful of elite runners maybe, some corporate types who want to make sure they're getting some bang from their sponsorship bucks, and, I suppose, those who, like me, want to remember.

It's an odd experience for me. First, the sight of that great mob of people at the start always brings tears to my eyes, and then as I watch the screen, the coffee in my mouth turns sour. I know what causes this. It's the memory of chemotherapy. That metallic taste that sits on the edge of your tongue like cheap diet cola. Chemo gave everything that taste. Occasionally I would eat huge meals and have no recollection of any flavor. Except perhaps the burned-out sense of an empty room the morning after a party.

I watch marathons to make sure I never forget.

Chemo gave me so many sensations. Nausea from the Adriamycin; blinding headaches from the Cytoxan; bowel cramps from the vincristine; and the endless chemically induced depression from the prednisone. I would stagger from the doctor's office feeling as though the side effects of all the drugs I'd ever used or thought of in the 1960s were running wild through my body.

I ran a marathon on chemo. I was running for my life.

I started running to combat the knowledge that my life was being stolen from me. I ran to beat the cancer of depression and the depression of cancer. Actually the word *running* is hyperbole; in this case ambling was closer to reality. I would shamble down the hill and back, probably ten minutes of motion, but it gave me the sense of doing something for myself. Gradually I built up to running a couple of miles three or four times a week. As I puffed along the top of Mulholland Drive, I would gulp down deep drafts of air in the belief that the oxygen was making its way into my bloodstream on a mission of mercy.

I would visualize all those good oxygen molecules pushing up my white count and fighting off the desecration of those wily little cancer cells. One day it struck me that perhaps I shouldn't be doing this much exercise. After all, those were pretty vicious drugs they were pumping into me. What if I was helping destroy myself with this running business? I brought it up with my doctor. He asked me if I thought it helped. I told him yes. He said that anything that made me feel better was fine with him, but to take it easy.

"Don't overdo it," was his advice.

Later that day I sent off an application for the Los Angeles Marathon and I never told him until after it was over.

I had always wanted to run a marathon and now two days before my fiftieth birthday, I found myself trudging along accompanied by the grunts, fart, and sweat of twenty-five thousand people of all races, creeds, and colors. All of us embarked upon our various odysseys, some to win, some to merely finish. In their eyes could be seen the flicker of lost youth, abandoned love, or sheer desperation. It occurred to me that my reasons for putting myself through this torture were just as varied as those of the rest of this jiggling mass of flesh that was struggling through the dog vomit landscape of Los Angeles with its sun-bleached streets and empty-eyed houses that marked our passage. And, as the awful reality of running 26.2 miles gradually wore down what little strength I possessed, I considered quitting.

In the twenty-second mile I was a mere shadow of my former shell. The sound of my breath seemed too much to take. I noticed I was weaving. It was then that I heard my name.

"Nick, Nick."

I wiped the sweat off my forehead and looked around. There on the sidewalk about thirty feet ahead of me, jumping up and down, was a heavyset African American woman.

"Nick!" she yelled, waving her arms to catch my attention.

I recognized her. Her name was Pat. She had recovered from breast cancer and had been part of the support group that I attended during the past year. I hadn't seen her for a couple of months and now here she was, screaming out my name with a beatific smile on her face. Her excitement at finding me pumped me up. My head came back and my chest went out.

"That's Nick," she shouted at a boisterous looking group of young black men, "he's baaad!" I was immediately acceptable. Smiles appeared and the men broke into whoops and hollers. They pumped their fists into the air.

"Go Nick! Go Nick!" they chanted and I, as a nonathletic white man at the end of his forty-ninth year, was pathetically grateful. Tears came into my eyes, while I surreptitiously checked that my fellow runners were aware of how hip I was to have such cool supporters. I shot them all a big smile and swerved across the road to high-five Pat. Their voices fell behind me and after the rush of adrenaline ebbed away, once again I was stumbling along, praying for it to end. And suddenly it did. I turned a corner and there it was. Flags and crowds, officials lining the way into the roped-off chutes, the digital time clock ticking away second by second and, in the background, the roar of the crowd. I was aware of the pounding of blood in my ears, the momentary relief of a breeze that touched my temples.

I was caught by an inane competitive spirit that pushed me forward to overtake three people in the last twenty yards, and then, the ineffable delight of crossing the finishing line. I am ecstatic, gloriously alive, golden. I think: *If I can do this what chance does cancer have?*

I saw my life stretch out ahead of me as though I'd opened a door in a darkened room to reveal blue skies and endless prairie. Way out in front it stretched, and for that moment I was completely happy, even though I know it only required the one word, *cancer*, to snap it back again.

NICK ULLETT is a writer-actor. He has done everything from the Ed Sullivan Show to creating the role of Gerald in the Broadway musical *Me and My Girl*. He's been an NPR commentator, had several plays produced, sold TV scripts and films, and his one man show, *Laughing Matters*, was highly acclaimed when it opened the season for Primary Stages in New York. He is at work on a novel. But then, who isn't?

The Way to Fill
a Sunday Afternoon

Suzanne Schryver

Sunday afternoon stretched out long and lonely on the lazy breezes of spring. Sunlight poured through the few windows I had on the front and back of my townhouse-style apartment. Sunlight that beckoned, calling me out to play. But it was Sunday afternoon, and no one was around to play.

Since moving to northern California six months earlier, I had made a few friends through work, church, a new hobby of karate, and running. In my first days in my new town, I had joined a group of runners who frequently trained together, and some of us had grown to be friends.

But today, as was frequent on nonrace weekends, we had all gone our separate ways. The weekend was mine to fill as I could. First, I thought, I'd go for a run; take care of my need for exercise. I pulled on a pair of running shorts, threw on a singlet, and tied my shoes. I had a choice of running in my neighborhood, which was limited to square blocks of various sizes, or going elsewhere. This afternoon, I was looking for something more serene and out of the way. I grabbed my wallet and keys.

I headed for the Sacramento River Trail, which wound its way alongside the river, across a footbridge, and back on the river's east side. The tail end would pull me through a residential area and over a well-traveled auto bridge back to the small parking lot. Six miles from start to finish, and I was up for it today. My typical distance was four or five miles, but I felt like pushing myself.

I locked my car, tucked my key into the pocket velcroed to my shoe lace, did a quick stretch, and I was off. My feet pounded the pavement, sending shocks of impact through my body. My breathing was rough in my throat, tight in my chest, and loud to my ears as it entered and exited my partially open mouth. Maybe I wouldn't make the six miles after all. The dry California air always seemed to scorch my lungs, and no matter how much I ran, I could not get used to that sharpness.

The trail was wide for the first mile. I passed several people out on their Sunday walk. I saw a woman with her sister or a friend—I wasn't certain which—and two small children who found great intrigue in clambering over the rocks to the river's edge to watch the water passing by. A lone rollerblader, or two, passed on their day's recreation. One bold biker flew by, veering around me at the last second.

Before long, the rhythm of my feet on the pavement had lulled me into a routine that was familiar. My breathing relaxed with the effort of my body, and I fell into the muscle memory of the run. The trail narrowed, the foot traffic diminished, and I was alone.

The smells of manzanita and eucalyptus mingled sweet and sharp in the air. These were the very smells that I had come to associate with my new home. My mind began to wander back to the journey that had brought me to California from teaching at a small, private boarding school back east. I thought of Sundays and childhood and big Sunday dinners in the middle of the afternoon. I wondered what my family and friends were doing right now, three hours later in their day.

The noise of an engine reached my ears from up the river, not a noise I'd ever heard this far out. I was on a footpath, too narrow for a vehicle to travel. I ran on, maintaining perfect cadence. At the footbridge, I glanced up the river to see a dump truck dumping hundreds of bright yellow rubber ducks into the moving water. Of course, I remembered. Today was the annual duck race for charity. The little creatures bobbed frantically as they vied for position.

Meanwhile, I took a hard right off the bridge, down into a dip then up again. My body was light and my movements were fluent. In front of me, my shadow danced on the pavement. She was an angel floating on ahead, tugging me by the soles of my feet, urging me to follow and not stop.

Wildflowers dotted the riverbank, as bright as the ducks spotting the river's surface. How strange, I thought, to dump foreign objects into a river in the name of charity. I hoped someone was going to come through and make sure none got stuck along the way. And I hoped it was the person who had come up with the idea. I ran on, secure in the knowledge that I'd easily beat at least a handful of straggling ducks down the river.

In front of me, the gate leading off the trail and into the neighborhood was visible. *That can't be,* I thought, glancing at my watch. *I haven't run five and a half miles already.* My watch told me I was wrong. *But I'm not ready to stop,* my mind whined as I flew through the narrow gate keeping my elbows close to my body.

On a whim, I turned around, never breaking my pace. My breathing was easy, and my legs were relaxed. I felt like I could run forever. Back down the trail I flew, the angel that was my shadow pushing from behind this time. But I noticed no difference. My feet sailed, barely touching the pavement, making no impact to jar my body. The run was smooth. Smooth as the front-runner ducks skimming the surface of the water.

My thoughts wandered from one idea to the next. I came up with ideas for stories I would write. I solved issues I was having with my students. I dealt with my own emotional loneliness. I prayed for guidance. I was all mind now. Through the rhythm of my exertion, I had transcended the physical. If I picked up my feet, I could soar four feet above the trail, gliding like the eagles circling in the sky. I was free from the bounds of gravity, from the laws that bound ordinary people to the earth.

My path widened again and became more populated. I had just taken a trip from the city far into the wilderness where only the most brave travel. I had gone to a place that few people ever experience. But as with all journeys, I now had to return to civilization, return to being the Suzanne who had to go to work in the morning and pay her rent every month. I would once again be the Suzanne who felt a pang of loneliness at being so far from family and friends.

And as my run wound down, so did my pace. I began to feel the miles that I had traveled, not just as a long run, but as blisters on my toes and the balls of my feet. As muscles that were stiff and weary from exertion beyond what they'd known before. As lungs that would feel just a bit tighter than usual for the rest of the day.

I stopped finally, and did a cool-down walk and a long stretch. My heart fluttered and my head spun with the knowledge that I had just completed eleven miles, the longest run—by several miles—that I had ever done. And until the very end, until my necessary return to civilization, it was effortless.

SUZANNE SCHRYVER has been an avid runner for seventeen years. She has published several short stories and is currently working on a novel. She lives in New Hampshire with her family.

Happy Heart Running

George Beinhorn

It's not every day a runner is blessed to skim over the ground effortlessly, feeling fast, happy, and free, especially when he's sixty years old.

It didn't start like that, or anything like it. It's Friday, and I felt more like sitting under a tree with a cool drink and a good book. Truth be told, I've been unhappy with my running lately. And it was all going so well—I was training at the right pace, doing the kind of running my body wanted on a given day, and feeling wonderful. Then I began listening to "the experts," and it all started going downhill. Soon, I was training too hard and all my runs were kind of average, and no single run was deeply satisfying.

I took a week of easy running to let my body recover while I reflected on my training and returned to the running that works best for me. But it took a whole week for the spring to return to my legs. And even then, though my body felt ready to run, in my mind there were lingering doubts. Could I get back to the thread of finely tuned training?

I set off from the stadium on the Stanford campus and jogged my usual warm-up route through the athletic complex, past the swimming pools, baseball and soccer fields, then proceeded out through the eucalyptus groves.

Before setting off, I had prayed deeply to know the right way to train. Then, during the warm-up, I prayed to run expansively. "I don't want to run for any other reason than to expand my heart," I said. "I don't want personal glory, or to run fast so that others will admire me. That's just stealing from them; I want to run to discover my heart and radiate love, kindness, and goodwill to all."

I warmed up for a very long time, deeply determined not to fall back into the trap of running too fast. I warmed up for a whole hour, keeping my heart rate at 65-70 percent of maximum. That's very slow, a mere shuffle, but I was determined not to run any faster unless and until my heart told me that it was right.

I spent the first forty minutes struggling with restless thoughts. I prayed for clarity, and then my heart began to feel relaxed and at peace. Jogging through the biology complex, I felt happy to be finding my rhythm, and an old Duke Ellington tune came cheerfully to mind: *"It don't mean a thing, if it ain't got that swing!"*

As my pace rose, I glanced at the monitor to see how much faster my heart was beating. I was running at a speed that would normally have raised my heart to 134-137 beats per minute, yet it was cruising at 123-127. What had happened? I wondered if the long warm-up had given my body time to settle in.

I thought about Bernd Heinrich's book *Why We Run: A Natural History*. In 1981, Heinrich decided to break the American record for 100 kilometers (62.2 miles). His choice of training methods was unique. He decided to train exclusively at race pace, or about six minutes per mile. "I made running my normal state," he wrote. Whenever he went shopping, he ran through the parking lot from the car to the store. This was in addition to his regular training, where he quickly advanced from fifteen to a hundred-plus miles per week, all at six-minute pace. A world-famous naturalist and a former successful collegiate runner, Heinrich tells how he modeled his training after animals that perform spectacular feats of endurance, such as migrating birds. After training heavily for a while, he noticed that he wasn't eating much more at a hundred miles per week than at fifteen, yet he'd lost very little weight. He decided that his body had become extremely efficient at metabolizing food for energy.

With my heart relaxing at 123-127 beats, running at a speed that would normally have raised it ten beats higher, I wondered if I hadn't accomplished something similar, and whether the long, slow warm-up had given my body the right exercise and sufficient time to become highly efficient.

An hour into the run, I felt relaxed and comfortable. My body felt as if it could easily run much faster, and so I let it accelerate a little bit. All the while, I was focusing my attention gently at the point between the eyebrows and talking to God, checking in to be sure that I would make the right decisions. I knew it would be all too easy to slip into fast running, and I steadfastly curbed the impulse. The ancient teachings of yoga say that the "spiritual eye" within the midpoint of the forehead is the "broadcasting station" for prayer, and that the heart is the intuitive "receiving station" for receiving the divine response. Interestingly, modern neuroscientists have discovered that the prefrontal cortex, just behind the forehead, is where such advanced abilities as concentration, perseverance, and positive, upbeat attitudes are localized in the brain, and that the anterior cingulate gyrus, a structure in the middle of the forehead, becomes electrically activated during deep states of meditation.

With the stopwatch at 1:02, I asked if I should run tempo or go long and slow. Receiving no clear answer, I decided I'd try some tempo and see if I could maintain the lovely feelings of harmony that I'd been enjoying.

I picked up the pace, and as my heart rate rose I checked the feelings in my heart, because I've discovered that I feel intuitive guidance most strongly there. As my heart rate passed 140, I noticed a distinct feeling of harmony, but as it climbed into the 150s the feeling vanished. I held pace at 150-155 for a few minutes, but then I thought, *If I don't drop back down to 140 and explore those feelings of harmony, I may be wasting an opportunity to learn something quite wonderful.*

I slowed until my heart fell back into the low 140s, and for the next three miles I held that pace and was rewarded by extraordinary, unbroken feelings of deep harmony and happiness in my heart.

Earlier, at the start of the run, I had had trouble finding a rhythm as I struggled to pull my thoughts together and raise my mood. But now a lovely, smooth rhythm came effortlessly. My body was poised over its center of gravity, while my feet padded lightly over the ground. My spine was straight, and my breathing came full and expansive, filling my upper body. My head was raised calmly, my eyes relaxed and looking ahead, not downward. My attention was strongly interiorized—I had no trouble keeping my mind focused, even though I was running on a paved road where cars were whizzing by. It was pleasant to stay focused "inside" while the sights "out there" simply weren't very interesting to me. This was a delightful way to run, and the thought came irresistibly: *This is happy heart training.*

God had answered my prayer. Today I *knew* how to train. It felt so completely *right*, and the knowing had come through my heart, with undeniable certainty. I had run expansively, and the proof was that my heart was more than bodily and personally soothed. There were feelings of a love and joy that I discovered, later in the day, I could extend in silent blessing to others. I stopped at the market on the way home, and as I chatted with the checkout clerk, I noticed that my heart was deeply relaxed, gracious and appreciative.

An hour and a half into the run, I swung back through the campus, making a long S-curve across the front of the quad and turning east through the biology complex. My body had begun to tire, and it announced this by running more slowly at the same heart rate. That was fine; I felt no compulsion to run fast, whether for dignity or machismo. The heart's love was so all-sufficing that I simply didn't require anything else.

Earlier, during the first miles, I reflected that whenever I pray to God, He rarely "explains"—that is, He seldom answers through my mind. Instead, the answers come through my heart. If I pray with one-pointed attention, from my deepest, most honest need, the response always comes. It can be a little puzzling if I don't get the answer right away, but if I carry on, and really mean business with God, I suddenly find that in some strange and subtle way, I *know*.

That's what happened today. God didn't explain, but I *knew*. I knew to start running tempo, and I knew how fast to run. Then there was a fleeting, wonderful sensation of harmony in my heart when it passed 140, as if to say: *That's it!* And finally, the confirmation, with miles of wonderful running in a state of primal happiness, with my heart bathed in love. Afterward, there was the proof—my body had worked hard, doing *good training*, and as I sang to God on the way home, my spirit resounded deeply through my heart.

It was in many respects a perfect run. It was excellent training, it was mentally healing, and it was spiritually blessed. Maybe God didn't talk to me in words, but He answered my prayers.

GEORGE BEINHORN has been a runner since 1969. His website is www.fitnessintuition.com.

Running in Circles

Chris Armstrong

It was one of those years. You've had 'em. Everyone has. What to do? Spontaneous combustion just wasn't an option. Alcohol was out—I tend to fall asleep, which does serve a purpose, but then there is the whole waking-up part. Gambling is too, well, intermittent. Why not running? It helped before. So I ran. And ran. And ran. Some days I almost ran out of road. And the strangest thing happened . . .

I met myself on the road. Swimming in cacophany, I first focused on finding my beat, my rhythm, *my* pace. The static turned to white noise, and suddenly, the whole became greater than the sum of its parts, and the symphony that is me could run forever. So I did. Then I heard a high note, reached out and grabbed it, and lo and behold! I remembered the melody of my nearly forgotten dreams, humor, imagination, sense of wonder, my heart of hearts, my very soul. Ideas would magically pop into my head. Time ran differently, delightfully. My morning runs quickly became my meditation, inspiration, and guaranteed delicious date with myself.

Then I met the world. For the finest dawn run, one must get to know night, so I did. (Well, me, my headlamp, pepper spray, and Diamond, my German shepherd/Siberian husky mix.) I whispered secrets with the moon, and watched it set. I winked back at stars, sang with them, and watched them fall. Then sun pokes its head through the stage curtains, checking out the audience before bursting onto the stage, and the blazing Gone-with-the-Wind colors take my breath away. Sweet light follows, and the land is slathered in butter and honey. And the seasons! During the eager green of spring, I have run in the silence of a cloud, become heady with the elixir of freshly turned earth, and felt a thousand angel kisses of mist on my face. (By the way, rain on glasses is nearly kaleidoscopic—try it!) During the riots of summer, I have breathed deeply the aroma of newly mown grass and fresh laundry, flowers bloom before me as I run, and clouds have been my pacesetter. Yes, I've reveled with storms, resonated with thunder, and danced with lightning. When the classic palette of autumn prevails, the trees and I bow our "good mornings," the perfume is musk of leaves with smoky undertones, and the sun wraps its beams around me and squeezes. I've even made friends with steel-blue winter (well, me, polypro, and Gore-Tex Windstopper), spinning and sparkling with snowflakes, tilting my head to receive the caresses of the breeze on my cheek, and basking in the moonlight reflecting off snow. I've run with the wind, thanking it for the push. I've run against the wind, thanking it for making me strong. I *always* thank it for the smell of pancakes with maple syrup it brings, and for carrying my messages on its wings.

I've scalloped with goldfinches, run with a jet on my wing, and coveted its jet stream, and heard the murmurings of monarchs' one thought: *Find home, find home, find home . . .* I've passed beachcombers, a Tai Chi class, people standing on their heads, sharing a dance step with a friend, setting up play dates for their dogs. Heartland farmers wave, Thai monks *wai*, and Tahitian fishermen murmur "Bonjour." I've run along the Magnificent Mile, the Gold Coast, and the Sea of the Moon. The mundane became sacred.

Rocks become Stonehenge. Each bead of dew is a crystal ball. I've contemplated "what ifs" as I've run past shrines, temples, churches, and ruins. What if the winds rippling the grasses are just another form of waves? What if the sky were the ground, and I was running on the sky? What if I am a fish, looking at the sun pour through a hole in the clouds as if it were a hole in the ice? And deeper things.

And I met God. (Dear Reader—That's what I call Him, please feel free to substitute your own personal paradigm.) After learning to ask for solutions and having them miraculously appear, I started saying "Thank you." Since then, He's also revealed how to trust (ever caught a breeze right when you needed one?), be patient (got to get through the first half of the run to get to that glorious second half), and appreciate nuances (aka layering) and contrasts (cool water tastes like nectar after a hot day's run). God and I banter and joke. On a day when I was feeling particularly unloved, I asked for a sign. The East started to lighten, turned hot pink. The pink slowly spread north and south, until it was 360-pink. I felt arms around me. So naturally, the next unloved time, I dared him to do it again. The east got pink, and it spread, but it just didn't get all the way around. Oh, man! I knew it. Then suddenly, the pink grew, rippled, then galloped right over my head, across the top! Imagine someone running their hand from your forehead, over the top of your head, down your back. *Then* arms all the way around. He *does* have a sense of humor! Another day he revealed that the prayers of others for me create a shield that I have relied upon yet taken for granted for all of my life. I was deeply humbled. Every day I praise, petition, reconcile, but mostly still say again and again, "Thank you, thank you, thank you."

Do you get it? Children do, but they are closer to it. If you don't, I can't explain it. But you probably run, and you've read this far, so this just puts words to what the very fibers of your being already know.

There have been lows. I have tasted dust. I have encountered dogs so large they were visible by satellite. My heart has ached with the staggering beauty of leaping deer, and the knowledge that only some of us may see spring. I have raged, yearned, and bargained to no avail. I have asked "why" more than once. My tears have mixed with raindrops, as if God and I were crying together. Sometimes, I remember . . . it was the lows that got me out there in the first place, that spurred me on. Without them, I would never had discovered all of the above and more, blazed the trail, been galvanized, had my eyes open enough to see all that God has revealed to me. So me and the morning sun skip across the grasses/amber waves/whitecaps/drifts, rise up the church spires/mountain peaks/pines/skyscrapers, kiss the tops of their heads, that touch the sky, that touches . . . you.

So I've come full circle, in a double helix kind of way: The more I know God, the more I know the world and myself, and vice versa. I understand now that I am a conduit, a prism—the Light passes through me, and the best I can do is to run with the wind, let the veils go, and stay transparent so that I can show you a rainbow.

CHRIS ARMSTRONG Aunt bookbinder curious daughter eclectic friend gatherer hardy intrinsic juris doctor kinetic listener mentor mother nebula observer painter quixotic reader seeker sister superconductive traveler trust officer ubiquitous voracious wife xenogamous yankee in the zone.

Knowing Running

David Talbird

Running sometimes imitates my spirituality. Or maybe it's my spirituality that imitates running. Ever since I became a runner at the age of fourteen I have been devout in my running at times, but at others I stray. Running has always been there whether I care to acknowledge it or not. It sustains me even when I curse it. It doesn't get jealous when I neglect it, but it never stops reminding of its presence. When I do return, the roads and trails always welcome me back with open arms. I'm like the prodigal son returning to the home that I've abandoned. Whether I go to church or not, I will still be considered a Christian. In the same way, whether I am running or not, I am still considered a runner.

People ask me if I enjoy running. They tell me that I'm not going anywhere. It seems monotonous. I'm not using it as a mode of transportation, so what's the use? There is just no end. When I am a devoted runner, I smile and tell them simply that it is the journey that fulfills me. I have never *arrived* in my quest to find God. To stay static in my beliefs is to lose touch with a powerful and dynamic spiritual experience. To arrive at some final point in my running is similar. In fact, running is my spiritual journey. I find myself much closer to a spiritual awakening in my best moments as a runner than I do within the walls of a holy building. When I am burned out and turn my back to my running I may tell people that it is boring and monotonous. You may hear that I only did it because I excelled and received a college scholarship for it. I deceive others when I say this, though, because I know deep down something that they don't. I know that I love it. I know that I will be back on the roads eventually.

I may have never walked alongside God, but I sure have felt like I've run with Him. There aren't enough words on this Earth to describe the feeling that you get when you hit what is sometimes known as the runner's high. The label does so little justice to the actual feeling. I sometimes wonder if it resembles the feeling of inner peace that Buddhist monks strive to achieve their whole life. Now, just because I have experienced it doesn't mean that I know how to achieve it. Nor does it mean that I always feel like it is worth the work and dedication required to achieve the feeling.

As I'm recalling the moments, I begin to tear up as I write this down. Some may wonder why. To tell you exactly why, though, would be like describing God. I can attempt to, but then I only limit the spiritual experience to my words. The feeling quickly fades and the experience merely becomes marks on paper.

When I go back to that emotional experience, I have to quit trying to describe it, but just feel it. At those moments I can smell the world around me. My steady breathing becomes silent next to the wind rushing past my ears. Goose bumps begin to form on my arms; my pace quickens. I know that I'm going faster, but it doesn't hurt. It doesn't even take any extra effort. At this moment I am conscious of every movement of my body from my blistered toes all the way to the sweat rolling down my shaven head, but at the same time I don't feel anything at all. My conscious feels like it has become one with creation itself and the faster I run the more I abandon my humanly body and mind for nirvana.

My pace continues to quicken and the work I put in on a daily basis leaves my mind. The time I devote to running becomes time well spent on the most pleasurable activity in my life. I no longer look down at my watch. On a fall day brown, red, yellow, and orange paintings form before my eyes as I run along the canvas. My body warms all over from the inside out. A smile broadens on my face, as I know this feeling. I've lived this moment before during a run. All sorts of feelings bubble up from under my skin. They could be endorphins or adrenaline or the spirit within lifting me up, but I don't care to know why. I am living the moment. My thoughts flash to a church where men and women jump up and shout the name of the Lord as they dance around. These public displays I have snickered at suddenly become comprehensible. I am feeling the internal tremor they must have experienced. Suddenly words come out of my mouth. I hear a "Thank you" echo through the trees. A conversation ensues where I describe how much I love to run. Words of encouragement shower me discussing goals for the year. I hear a five-mile time that seems all too attainable even though just days before I remember settling on a much slower and *realistic* time after a poor race. I hear "Let's go" with every exhalation of breath as I now consciously increase my pace and lengthen my stride. I no longer know if I'm talking to myself or if there is someone else having this discussion with me.

Someone may be able to explain this high and what actually is happening to my body physiologically. They may explain it in a perfectly logical and scientific manner that seems to take away from its mysterious nature. It doesn't matter to me. Nothing you tell me will diminish the spiritual experience I feel. I can only imagine that those who try to explain it away are those who could never experience it. I am convinced that it is a humbling spiritual experience and that it comes from deep within. It will come only to those who love running. It won't happen if you merely run to keep in shape as if it's a chore. You can never force it to happen.

The phenomenon known as the runner's high has pushed me toward incredible workouts where I recall the time and effort required for the distance, and it amazes me still. This particular time I have a different reaction. I've been here before, and today I just stop. Stop in the middle of the forest trail. I have the biggest smile on my face and feel the excitement of a child on Christmas morning. I look in all directions to tell someone. I want to tell them about it. If I see anyone, I don't know what I will say. They might think I'm crazy, but I'd probably tell them the only thing I could say. *I know.* What do I know? How do I know? Why do I think I know? These are all trivial questions limited to a human vocabulary. They only take me away from understanding. This is the closest to heaven I've ever been. The road is a long and narrow one, and I couldn't tell you how to get there, but I do know it exists. I sit down on a log a little removed from the trail. I wish that I could relate even a tiny bit of what I feel at these times. I sit with that grin and tears begin to form. If you've ever felt this you won't have to ask why I react the way I do. You know.

DAVID TALBIRD lives in Arlington, Virginia, writing and studying in his spare time. He is attempting to launch his website, TheRetraction.com, to encourage creative thinking and discussions about the world around us. He still runs, and wants to run his first marathon from Marathon to Athens, Greece.

Finding My Way to High

Mary Z. Fuka

I remember what the high felt like. How, deep into a long run, my mind would slip its mooring from conventional space and time and slide into a dimension a half step beyond. I remember the simple astonishment at how the push, the pounding, the sheer effort of running had sublimated somehow into a delicious athletic beatitude, every footfall a benediction upon the earth returned ten-thousand-fold. If it was running making me feel like that, I was inclined to keep doing it so that I never felt any other way, engraving an infinite loop into my running soul.

As a runner I am not, nor have I ever been, anything special. My build is broad-hipped and chesty, emphatically earthbound. It seems surpassingly odd that I would have ever had a talent for achieving ecstasy through running. Maybe it was some trick of the Fates to compensate for a spectacular lack of any talent beyond a certain endurance native to my stocky peasant frame. Whatever the reason, after a few miles on a trail I could segue into euphoria as smoothly as my fast and powerful racing friends could turn on the afterburners coming into a finish line. It was a revelation to me that more obviously deserving runners might experience a runner's high only rarely if at all. My running joy came to my bidding like a silken scarf to a magician's hand. It was my peculiar and beloved boon.

Not anymore. It has been a long, long time since I could run hard enough and far enough to catch the high, a long, long time since I stepped from this dimension to the next. Now I am starting over as a runner, an old hand's mind in a newbie's body, an uncomfortable conjunction of eager spirit and less willing flesh. My feet thud upon rather than bless the ground. My running efforts are prosaic rather than transforming. Some days I come home content, with at least a sense of a job well done and some progress toward my former running self. Some days I come home tired. Some days I come home angry and exasperated at my athletic inadequacy. I am a runner redux, chasing after a mere state of mind, an ephemeral wisp of an overactive imagination. The high is out there somewhere, a shadowed beacon I glimpse only at intervals in my struggle to bring the expectations of experience in line with my current physical reality. I am Ahab, and the runner's high is my monstrous whale.

I live and run now in Boulder, Colorado, a city renowned for blissed-out endorphin junkies of all stripes, but especially for those addicted to running. Runners are everywhere here in endless happy variety. Elite runners as light as whippets blasting by, serious runners with their serious dogs trotting in disciplined fashion slightly ahead or slightly behind, lovely college girls all legs up to their collarbones and their good-looking V-shaped boys in tight formation, relaxed new-age runners who seem to barely touch the ground, new parents pushing babies in running strollers, men and women with my same extra few pounds deceptively running ever so much faster than I, kids bouncing back and forth between their moms and dads and dogs, grad students tossing ideas to and fro across the trail. I once saw a pair of Buddhist monks pacing along in their bright yellow-orange robes above Chatauqua, with shaved heads and remarkably wide grins, outmatching the sunflowers in their bright-burnished cheer.

I lean slightly into the faint breeze left as each runner or group of runners passes, snuffling deeply of their wakes, as avid for a stray endorphin as an ex-smoker for the second hand scent of cigarettes. I imagine secret running ecstasies behind every expression, however bland. I am the unwilling designated driver at a vast party where the drug of choice is good to you, good for you, and absolutely, fabulously free. I run on through the limbo-land between the runner I was and the runner I will be, following the faint spoor of remembered sensation.

There are any number of rational reasons to return to running. Fitness and health, the activity of mind that follows that of the body, the sense of mental and physical well-being, fresh air and regular sleep, the camaraderie of the running club, satisfaction of the competitive urge, whatever. Yet it is the irrational that draws me. The high has become the Shangri-la of my runner's mind. I recall that such a place exists, and that it is infinitely good, but I seem to have forgotten my way back. I don't think I understood back then as I understand now that a Shangri-la neglected folds in upon and hides itself. The path remains open only if it is well trod by feet eager for the journey and the destination. Why ever did I leave? Why does any runner stop running? Life gets in the way, we think. We become complacent about the rewards that seemed so trivially obtained. We wander onto darker roads only to find that the true path has become overgrown in the meantime and that we have lost our way.

It is time to clear the path and set my feet to running. Back to Shangri-la. Back to the runner's high.

MARY Z. FUKA is a physicist in Boulder, Colorado working on new methods to treat heart disease. She has spent her running life in the high deserts and peaks of the Rocky Mountain West discovering and rediscovering just how much fun it is to travel the trails at a pace that is, at best, an entirely insignificant fraction of the speed of light.

Morning in the
Garden of the Gods

Gerald C. Matics

I had been out of school and running on my own for two years
when I had my athletic epiphany. I had flown to Colorado with my
girlfriend that summer to visit her brother and see some of what
Woody Guthrie told me was my land. Part of the time we stayed in a
quaint Victorian bed-and-breakfast nestled at the foot of Pike's Peak,
just outside Colorado Springs.

When I found out where we were staying I flirted briefly with the
idea of running up the mountain. It would be something to tell my
nonrunning friends, at least, how I ascended one of the tallest mountains in the U.S., step by arduous step—conveniently leaving out the
fact that a stolid group of runners race a marathon up Pike's Peak
each year.

I scrapped the idea forthwith. I was a pretty good track runner in
college, not by any definition a great one. I'd won my share of races,
but I lost more often, and never finished first at a distance longer
than five kilometers. Now, like many postcollegiate athletes, I was
gradually eliminating "collegiate" from that description; my workouts
were slowly tailing off, and while I still contorted my schedule in an
effort to get my daily run in, it no longer bothered me unreasonably

if I didn't. I could still hold my own on the relatively flat suburban Philadelphia streets where I lived, but scaling a mountain at 6:30 per mile appealed to me about as much as plantar warts.

All of this is to say I was not on the razor's edge of conditioning on this trip, something I'd confirmed the day before in Denver, when I had my first taste of altitude training. It did not go well. I slogged through a hot, miserable five miles, gasping for breath and nursing a stitch and questioning the wisdom of running on vacation in the first place.

To this ordeal I would tack on an extra fifteen hundred feet of elevation for the next day's outing. What fun. Like the ghosts stamped on your eyes by a flash camera, the remnants of the stitch lingered the following morning at six when I groaned my way out of bed and groped for my running shoes. I abhor few things in life more than morning runs—voluntarily leaving the comfort of a bed to flagellate oneself seems somehow sacrilegious to me—but today it was the only time I would have. Mumbling something to my girlfriend about keeping a St. Bernard on standby, I trudged down the steps for the front door.

On the way I passed a rack of brochures hawking local attractions, and one touting the "Garden of the Gods" caught my eye. I looked it over more to postpone the inevitable than anything else, saw some pretty pictures of big rocks, discovered it was only a few minutes away from where we were, and decided to give the place a try. I'd drive the rental there, of course; it was only a mile away, but I didn't want to waste precious breath getting there and back.

Like a cartoon character, my jaw dropped when I got out of the car. I think the word that sounded in my mind was *majestic*. "Garden of the Gods" was apt, I was forced to admit.

The Garden of the Gods is a stunning collection of massive red-rock formations joined by a series of trails to which pictures in a brochure cannot do justice. Bright orange spires jut out of the earth at impossible angles and heights, beckoning toward the sky. Horse trails and hiking paths meander among the monoliths, inviting closer inspection.

I'd certainly be inspecting part of them, at any rate.

After some light stretching, I set off. The stitch was still nagging, and my legs were alarmingly stiff, probably from oxygen starvation, but I felt better than I'd expected. I roamed the flats for a while, ducking in and out of rock groupings, and still felt pretty good, so I tentatively approached a gradual hill.

At least, it was gradual when I started. The grade increased, and I had to decide whether it was worth the additional effort. Screw it, I thought, I used to be tougher than this. Lifting and driving like I'd been taught by my coaches what seemed like a hundred years before, I leaned into a hill the likes of which are rarely seen outside four-wheel-drive commercials. When the trail narrowed abruptly a minute later, I glanced up—and was floored by the sight. Spread out before me was most of the garden. The still-rising sun cast an incredible glow against the sheer rock faces. Paths that had seemed incoherently random from ground level took on complex patterns from my vantage eighty or more feet above, and I still had farther to climb. Overhead, clouds raced by, making shadow pools on the ground below.

I climbed higher, picking my steps carefully as I skipped among the stones on the path. Too bad I hadn't brought my camera, I thought. Of course I could always come back later, but this light could not last. I felt wonderfully strange. Before and since that day, I have had nearly every imaginable experience running. I've run in dozens of states and three foreign countries. I've run in front of crowds of forty thousand at the Penn Relays and raced a world champion in front of a couple of dozen curious track walkers at an informal, hush-hush summer meet. I've run during a hurricane. I've run drunk at two in the morning. I've run seven floors underground at the Princeton University fieldhouse and around the decks of a ship in the middle of the Caribbean Sea. But I have never experienced what I felt that day: a sort of affirmation of the proverbial Higher Power.

My step was light and springy; my shoes, my constant companions long past retirement age, had sprouted wings. I no longer felt anchored to earth. A thigh-busting, lung-searing ascent was some-how no more difficult than a gently rolling slope, and I was actually disappointed when I ran out of trail.

Turned out I wouldn't need the camera after all, I thought as I sur-veyed the magnificent vista; my heightened senses were recording every fine detail. For the first time in my running career, I knew for certain I was experiencing the fabled runner's high.

I looked below for a long time. Boulders were strewn like a child's playthings about the valley floor, surrounded by patches of trees and vegetation I in my eastern suburban ignorance could scarcely iden-tify. It struck me that these spectacular sights were eons in the mak-ing. I felt I could run, if not forever, for a mighty long time.

Then I turned around. Like Atlas on the horizon, Pike's Peak tow-ered in the distance. The sun behind me played some trick with the air, and I thought I saw a prism of colors bathe the land in between. Somewhere high up on that mountain, I knew, somewhere much higher than where I stood, in the death-heat of August, snow held its ground. I could not have been more awed had Handel's *Messiah* erupted from the stones around me. Eventually it was time to make my way back.

Altogether by the time I'd finished I had covered probably ten miles, double my daily average, although I felt fresher than when I'd set out. My body tingled like a live wire, and although I poked and prodded my side, there was no trace of the nagging stitch.

In the car on the way back, I digested what I felt. Not being a complete fool, I knew the Garden of the Gods held no miraculous power to make me a better athlete; there would still be tough days, and even had I beheld Yahweh himself at the summit of the mountain, I'd likely never look forward to peeling back the covers on a foggy gray morning to stumble through the empty streets. But I would take a piece of this incredible place home with me, and take it out to look at on those mornings, and maybe, just maybe, run easier for it.

My girlfriend was on the porch sipping coffee and reading when I got back. "I was about to send that St. Bernard," she said as I climbed the porch steps. "Good run?"

"Not bad," I told her, and went inside to shower.

Writer and editor GERALD C. MATICS lives in suburban Philadelphia with his wife, Lisa, and son, Jack. A former 4:12 miler, Gerald recently completed work on a running-themed novel, his first.

Penitentiary

Robert Padilla

CSP, or Colorado State Penitentiary, is about as somber and depressing an existence as you're going to get. It's a maximum-security prison cradled in the arid foothills of southern Colorado. A five-story red brick structure housing seven hundred and fifty very restless inmates confined to eight-foot-by-twelve-foot concrete boxes for twenty-three hours a day; sometimes for years on end.

It probably goes without saying that recreational diversions are extremely limited. The residents of this joint will usually wake up and turn on a twelve-inch TV they have sitting on their desk, confining themselves even further with images of a life out of reach. Images pumped in to pacify restless minds. Or they might stand at the front of their cells and try to pass the monotonous hours conversing with other inmates by yelling through cracks in the side of the cell doors or through the ventilation system that spiderwebs from cell to cell. Still others try to pass their time a bit more productively; maybe reading or drawing. Whatever the means, the idea is just to get through it without losing your mind. The lucky ones find a routine they can live with; and the ones who can't, they pass the hours in misery. Either way you're embodied in a place that exemplifies confinement.

Five times a week the inmates are allowed out of their single-man cells for an hour at a time. A trap in the cell door is unlocked by a guard who instructs them to back up and stick their wrists through the opening. They are handcuffed behind their back and the door is opened. They are escorted to another cell where the process is reversed. This cell has two walls, which are made of inch-thick shatterproof glass, so the guards can observe your every movement. The cell is completely barren, except for a pull-up bar bolted to one wall, and two slats cut in the concrete back wall to allow the prisoners to peek out at a desolate lunar landscape.

Now, I don't want to give the impression this is about CSP. It's not. But I do want to convey the conditions in which one begins to realize the true value of freedom. This is about finding that freedom, even in the most stringent of circumstances.

I'm a man who's fought tooth and nail for his freedom. The oddest thing is that I've finally found it in the most unlikely of places. My whole life, it seems, has been spent running from one thing or another. When I was very young I developed a penchant for running away from home, and submerging myself in a criminal lifestyle. A string of other bad choices eventually landed me in the joint, where I continued to run, although now it was for much higher stakes. I escaped on three different occasions. So when they opened up CSP I was at the top of the list for placement in this new maximum-security facility.

When I got here I established a routine. I read educational books to build my mind, and followed a strict calisthenics regimen to build the body. I think a person, even—and maybe even more so—in these circumstances, should always strive to grow stronger. Not only mentally and physically, but also spiritually. Right?

For the longest time the spiritual aspect has eluded me. I ventured down a couple of different paths, to no avail, including meditation, which just didn't seem to fit me. I've done more than enough sitting for a lifetime. I decided not to worry about it, though, and just keep doing what I could on the mental and physical fronts. I figured that when the time was right it would come on its own.

A while back I was telling the guy in the cell next to me that I was having pain in my legs after my leg workouts. He asked what kind of exercises I was doing. I told him I was doing squats, walking lunges, and step-ups on my stool. He told me that instead of just jumping straight into the calisthenics I should do some stretching, then try running for five or ten minutes, to get the blood circulating in my legs real good. I followed his advice and the next day did some light stretching before starting my run. I began running in my cell rather than the recreation cage, as there's an extra foot or so in my cell. It doesn't seem like much, but it makes a big difference. I can get in four good strides from my bunk to the door before I have to turn around and head back. And, believe it or not, I can get a pretty good rhythm going.

In the beginning, I only ran for a few minutes at a time. It was only a warm-up thing. When I finished I'd be out of breath and holding my side. Little by little, though, I started increasing the time I spent on the warm-up; eventually, the running itself became the focal point of my workout, and the calisthenics only parenthetical. I wasn't out of breath after ten minutes, and my sides no longer hurt. It was exhilarating. It evolved into something I wanted to do more and more. I take that back—it was something I *needed* to do more and more. It was fulfilling something in me that I'd been missing for a very long time. It seems I'd found a spirituality in this most unlikely of places. Something mystical in four simple strides. Back and forth. Back and forth. One, two, three, four; one, two, three, four. The movement itself, combined with the breathing, becomes a sort of mantra in motion. My mind seems to somehow break free from its fetters and enter a state of nonlocality, if that makes any sense. When I touch that moment—generally around forty-five minutes into my run—the tranquility turns into an expansion, and the mind ceases to inhabit a location. It's like I'm a nimbus beyond myself. Beyond everything. Individuation, thought, place. Everything.

I've never run for the sheer joy of it and certainly never for hours at a time. It's always been something I did merely to evade, and, although the term *escape* may still apply to my running, in an abstract way it's much more than that. It's now metamorphosed into a completely different animal than it was before. I'm now running towards something. Not just freedom, which in itself is a golden thing, but toward a liberation. Toward that euphoria that overtakes me when I find that groove. For someone who finds it hard to sit still and meditate it's the perfect substitute. Stillness isn't necessarily dependent on lack of motion. Sometimes, movement itself proves the catalyst for transcending an unpleasant place.

It's hard for me to explain the effect running has had on my life. Conditions aren't what you'd call ideal. I mean, you're running on concrete that has absolutely no give, in shoes more suited for clog dancing; but I make do and am able to flourish in an environment intended to wilt the spirit rather than build it up. I don't want to go into how running has rehabilitated me. This isn't about that; but I've actually found a peace of mind. Something I'll carry with me when they finally open the gate and let me run out a completely free man. It's done more than anyone could ever ask of a lock and key. And for that, I'm grateful.

More running books from Breakaway:

(for ages 2-7)   (for ages 2-7)

Available in bookstores everywhere, or from Breakaway Books
(800) 548-4348   www.breakawaybooks.com